THE ONE HUNDRED

FROM AARON TO ZECHARIAH

JUSTIN MORRIS

THE ONE HUNDRED
FROM AARON TO ZECHARIAH

iUniverse books may be ordered through booksellers or by contacting:

iUniverse
1663 Liberty Drive
Bloomington, IN 47403
www.iuniverse.com
1-800-Authors (1-800-288-4677)

Because of the dynamic nature of the Internet, any web addresses or links contained in this book may have changed since publication and may no longer be valid. The views expressed in this work are solely those of the author and do not necessarily reflect the views of the publisher, and the publisher hereby disclaims any responsibility for them.

Any people depicted in stock imagery provided by Getty Images are models, and such images are being used for illustrative purposes only. Certain stock imagery © Getty Images.

Scripture quotations from the Holy Bible, King James Version (Authorized Version). First published in 1611. Quoted from the KJV Classic Reference Bible.

ISBN: 978-1-5320-9303-6 (sc)
ISBN: 978-1-5320-9302-9 (e)

Library of Congress Control Number: 2020903085

Print information available on the last page.

iUniverse rev. date: 02/18/2020

INTRODUCTION TO THE BOOK

I started putting this together November 2nd 2019 after I found and article in a book that mentioned brief descriptions of 100 people in the Bible. My thought was that each person needed to be investigated a little further than this so I started doing research and in doing so, I grew much closer to Christ by studying His word.

This is a very brief study into each person but more so then what I had found. This book is designed for you to dig deeper. To spark an interest into what I have started. I hope it works for you like it did for me.

One thing I noticed as I studied was that the Old Testament, it had much better records when it came to the genealogy of the people than the New Testament did. Scholars did way more speculating when it came to New Testament people then they did with Old Testament, but if you think about it, most people that are mentioned in the New Testament where born in either the first century BC or AD.

I hope you enjoy reading about each person. It may cause you to research them even further than I did. I spent between two to four hours on each person and enjoyed every minute. I truly hope you do more research but just realize, there are different opinions out there. I just tried to stick with the facts and used the Bible about 90% of the time.

My last but not final thought, I would like to think my wife

Anna for dealing with the long nights at the computer and for Pastor David Dechape from Moses Lake Alliance Church in Moses Lake, WA for clearing up a few things. The final transcript was sent in on the 17th of February 2020 to the publishers. What a journey.

> 2 Timothy 2:15 *Study to shew thyself approved unto God, a workman that needeth not to be ashamed, rightly dividing the word of truth.*

ACCREDITATION OF THE AUTHOR

Justin Morris has a Bachelor's of Science degree in Business Administration from POST University in Waterbury CT, which is his latest degree. He also has a degree in Biblical studies from Shiloh Bible Institute. He was licensed as a minister in 1992 through the Pentecostal Evangelical Church and Ordained in 1997 after completing his degree plan.

For the past 30 years Justin has been involved with youth ministry, taught Sunday school, been an Asst. Pastor in a few churches, led home bible groups and most of all, been involved on worship teams as a guitar player, bass player and drummer.

In January 2018, he became the President of the church after the President of five years stepped down due to health issues. Since then he has built the organization up with new ministers throughout the US and the world to include seven countries. Justin has a successful YouTube channel that teaches the facts about the Bible called "Pentecostal Evangelical Church". Each person you read about in this book is taught, in order on the videos. Visit the channel and follow along.

Old Testament

Aaron	Ishmael		
Abel	Jacob		
Abraham	Jeremiah		
Adam	Job		
Balaam	Jonah		
Bathsheba	Jonathan		
Belshazzar	Joseph		
Boaz	Joshua		
Cain	Josiah		
Caleb	Leah		
Cyrus	Melchizedek		
Daniel	Methuselah		
David	Miriam		
Deborah	Mordecai		
Eli	Moses		
Elijah	Naaman		
Elisha	Naomi		
Enoch	Nebuchadnezzar		
Esau	Nehemiah		
Ester	Noah		
Eve	Rachel		
Ezekiel	Rahab		
Ezra	Rebekah		
Gideon	Ruth		
Hagar	Samson		
Hannah	Samuel		
Hezekiah	Sarah		
Hosea	Saul		
Isaac	Solomon		
Isaiah	Zerubbabel		

New Testament

Ananias	Mary, the mother
Andrew	of Jesus
Apollos	Mary Magdalene
Barnabas	Mary, sister
Caiaphas	of Martha
Cornelius	Matthew
Elizabeth	Nathanael
Herod Antipas	Nicodemus
Herod the Great	Paul
James the Apostle	Peter
James the brother	Philemon
of Jesus	Philip the Apostle
John the Apostle	Philip the Evangelist
John the Baptist	Pilate
Joseph	Priscilla
Judas Iscariot	Silas
Lazarus	Stephen
Luke	Thomas
Lydia	Timothy
Mark	Titus
Martha	Zacchaeus
	Zechariah

Old Testament

PEOPLE

AARON

The name Aaron is of Hebrew origin meaning "mountain of strength". According to Numbers 26:59 and Exodus 28:1, Aaron was the older brother of Moses and younger brother of Miriam. He was born in 1574 BC to his parents Amram and Jochebed. They were Kohathites of the tribe of Levi. Aaron was the first high priest of Israel. Before going up on Mount Sinai, Aaron agreed to help Moses free God's people in Egypt. Aaron was to help his brother Moses by speaking to Pharaoh because Moses had a speech impediment. This was risky because they were going to walk into a hostile environment. He also had the same power that God gave Moses to perform miracles. Fast forward to Mount Sinai, God showed both Moses and Aaron new revelation at Israel's camp while at Sinai. They both were allowed to enter into God's Holy presence on Sinai (Ex 19:24; 24:9-10). Aaron and Moses were leader-participants in the covenant Yahweh made between Himself and the people of Israel. However, there was a break in Aaron's loyalty to God and Moses. Aaron told the people to build a golden calf to worship when Moses was on Mount Sinai receiving the Ten Commandments. (Ex 32:1-10) Aaron allowed peer pressure to take over. In spite of his sin, Aaron was restored to his position of high priest. In Numbers 33:38-39, Aaron went up on Mount Hor and died when he was 123 years old. Aaron's son Eleazar became High Priest.

ABEL

The name Abel means, a breath, or vanity. He was born around 3972 BC His hometown would have been outside of Eden which today would have been in the Middle East or better known as Iran or Iraq. According to Genesis 4:2, he was born after his brother Cain and he was a sheep keeper. In verse 3-4, when it was time to bring an offering to the Lord, Abel brought the firstborn of his flock and the Lord had respect for his offering. Because of Cain's jealously, Abel was also the first murder that took place and because he was righteous, he was the first in paradise. Abel's offering was accepted by God because it was a blood sacrifice. Blood had to be shed in order to forgive sins. Jesus looked at this as the first Martyr according to Matthew 23:35. He was the first shepherd in the Bible as well. He is also mentioned first in the Faith Hall of Fame in Hebrews 11:4 as declaring him a "righteous man". If Abel had any weaknesses, it would have been the fact that Cain overpowered him. Some would say he would have been naïve or too trusting but who knew? There was no reason not to trust Cain because there had never been a murder before and he was his brother. Why not trust him. I would have. As you study about Abel, you will see there isn't much mentioned about him but what we can see, he was a righteous man. He demonstrated what Christ did for us on the cross by taking his best and sacrificed it for his sins.

ABRAHAM

Abraham's name may be viewed either as meaning "father of many" in Hebrew or else as a contraction of ABRAMהֲמוֹן hamon meaning "many, multitude". He is also considered as the father of faith. The biblical patriarch Abraham was originally named Abram but God changed his name according to Genesis 17:5. Abraham was born 1996 BC. According to Genesis 25:7, he lived for 175 years. In his early years, Abraham lived in Mesopotamia before he moved into the promise land. His mother is never mentioned in the Bible and only hinted about her in the Torah. His father was Terah which was an idol-worshiper. He was 70 years old when Abraham was born. In Genesis 12:10-20, Abraham and his wife went to Egypt to live but before they got there, Abraham told his wife to lie and say she was his sister to save his life. He was afraid they would have killed him and kept her. He did this again in Chapter 20. In Genesis 17 Abraham was 99 when God declared his name: "Abraham" a father of all nations. God had given him His word that he would still have a son by Sarah. Which when they heard this, they both laughed at God. This showed God their disbelief. But they did have a son named Isaac. However, this wasn't Abraham's only son. He had a son with Sarah's slave named Hagar. His name was Ishmael. We will talk more about Ishmael later. Abraham was tested by God asking him to sacrifice Isaac and Abraham would have done it if God hadn't stopped him.

ADAM

Adam is the only person you will read about that actually did not have a birthday as far as being born of a mother other than Eve. He had a Father which is God and he was created perfect. He was created for one purpose only and that was to serve God. He actually talked to the Lord face to face, which we know this to be God the Son, Jesus Christ. God literally created him from the dust of the ground. Then God breathed life into him. (Genesis 2:7) According to Jeff A. Benner from Ancient Hebrew Research Center, the word/name Adam is a child root derived from the parent דם (dam) meaning, "blood". By placing the letter א in front of the parent root, the child root אדם (adam) is formed and is related in meaning to דם (dam). The Hebrew word אדמה (adamah) is the feminine form of אדם meaning "ground" (see Genesis 2:7). There is one other connection between adam and adamah as seen in Genesis 2:7 which states that "the adam" was formed out of the adamah. In the ancient Hebrew world, a person's name was not simply an identifier but descriptive of one's character. As Adam was formed out of the ground, his name identifies his origins. Adam lived 930 years according to Genesis 5:3. As far as children Adam had, Cain was born first. Then Abel and then Seth. According to Genesis 5:4, Adam had other sons and daughters but we're not sure the roll they played other than population of the earth.

BALAAM

Balaam means "the destruction of the people". He was born 1451 BC to Beor. According to Wayne Jackson from the Christian Courier, "Balaam is one of the great tragedies of the Old Testament. He was a Gentile prophet of God (cf. 2 Peter 2:15, 16) who lived at Pethor in Mesopotamia (Deuteronomy 23:4)." He was a wicked prophet but not a false prophet. Balaam heard from God; however, Balaam's heart was not right with God. He betraying Israel and led them astray. In case you still don't remember this guy, he was the one that God caused a donkey to speak to after Balaam hit the donkey three times. The donkey Balaam was riding, could see the angel in front of him and kept trying to go around but Balaam could not see it, and when the donkey three times moved to avoid the angel, Balaam was angry and beat the animal. "Then the Lord opened the donkey's mouth" (Num 22:28), and rebuked the prophet for the beatings. "Then the Lord opened Balaam's eyes, and he saw the angel of the Lord standing in the road with his sword drawn" (verse 31). The angel told Balaam that he certainly would have killed Balaam had not the donkey spared his life. The funny thing is, a dumb beast had more wisdom than God's prophet. Numbers 22-24. My thought is, why didn't Balaam take a step back when he heard the donkey speak? That would have got my attention if nothing else.

BATHSHEBA

The name Bathsheba means "daughter of the oath" in Hebrew. בַּת־שֶׁבַע The first time Bathsheba is mentioned in the bible is in 2 Sam 11:3. She is the daughter of Eliam and the wife of Uriah the Hittite. When her husband was away at war, she was bathing on the roof top, which was very common except this time. She had just finished her monthly cycle and was performing ceremonial bathing to be cleansed from her uncleanness according to 2 Sam 11:4 and king David happened to see her when he was on his roof top enjoying the night. He told his servants he wanted to see her. When she heard the news that king David wanted to see her, it is possible that she thought he had news about her husband or her father. Both of them were considered "Might Men" and were at war. She also had a grandfather by the name of Ahithophel. He was king David's chief advisor. To be very clear, the scripture 2 Sam 11:4 KJV says, "And David sent messengers, and took her;" which some suggests she was taken advantage of (Strong's 3947) in the original Hebrew "took" means seize, take captive, to be captured. Bathsheba lived in a time when women were looked upon as property. In this case, she might have thought if she refused, it could be bad for her husband. The common belief is she knew David would be out there and so she made sure she was there to.

BELSHAZZAR

His name in the Hebrew is בֵּלְשַׁאצַּר, Belshatsar, Greek Βαλτάζαρ, Baltázar, meaning "Bel protect the king". It is a prayer to the Babylonian god. It is believed he was around 40 years old when he became king. He was the last king of Babylon before the fall in 539 BC which would have put his birth year around 595 BC. Now the Hebrew word for king can also be interpreted as governor or royal prince and history records that he was both. Some say because of that fact, he wasn't a king at all. Belshazzar was Nebuchadnezzar's grandson through his daughter Nitocris. Belshazzar calls Nebuchadnezzar his "father" in Daniel 5:13, but this is a generic use of the word father, meaning "ancestor." Nabonidus, who ruled the empire of Babylon from 555-538 BC, mentions his firstborn son Belshazzar on an inscription found in the city of Ur in 1853. The inscription reads: "May it be that I, Nabonidus, king of Babylon, never fail you and may my firstborn, Belshazzar, worship you with all his heart." Another piece of evidence for Belshazzar's reign in the city of Babylon comes from an inscription where he is referred to as the son of Nabonidus and is given authority to rule according to biblehistory.net (2013). In Dan 5 Belshazzar was having a feast that mocked God. A finger wrote on the wall and Belshazzar became scared. Mene, Mene, Tekel, Upharsin. (25-28) He died that same night verse 30.

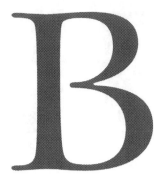

BOAZ

In the Hebrew he is known as "Ufiz", "Yu'ar", "Baath", "Boaz", בּוֹעַז
means "quickness". He was born 1250 BC in Bethlehem, Judah and
died the same place in 1050 BC. He was the son of Salmon and he
married Ruth. He was the father of Obed. He was a rich landowner
who noticed Ruth, the widowed Moabite daughter-in-law of Naomi,
a relative of his, gleaning grain from his fields. He finds out that her
and her family is poor and that Ruth has this devote loyalty to
Naomi. So, Boaz invites her to eat with him and his workers every
day and deliberately leaves grain for her to glean while keeping a
protective eye on her. Later on, down the road, He builds a
relationship with her and she asked him to marry her by uncovering
his feet while he was sleeping and laying crossways. He wakes up
and they have a conversation about getting married, but she had to
be freed from another first in 3:13. In 4:1-7 Boaz met with a close
relative and redeemed a piece of land and this gave the right to marry
Ruth. When you think about this story, you picture a very rich man
that wasn't afraid to give. He honored the Lord with his money. He
saw that Ruth was poor and that she had chosen to take care of
Naomi in her old age even after Ruth's husband, which was Naomi's
son, was dead. Ruth was far away from her people and didn't know
anyone, yet she stayed to care for Naomi and risked never having
children. Boaz heard from the Lord and moved.

CAIN

The name means "spear". Cain was the oldest from Adam and Eve. He also committed the first murder in human history by killing his brother Abel. Genesis 4:8 This was out of pure jealousy because God had accepted Abel's offering and not Cain's. We know that Cain was banished by God to the Land of Nod which was East of Eden (4:16). This scripture implies that he was even more separated from God because his fate was to live as a homeless guy. Like an outsider. He was worried that people would try to kill him so God gave him a sign of protection that if anyone killed him, that the Lord would avenge him sevenfold. The Hebrew word for Nod is לָנוּד which means exile or wonderer of even fugitive. After Cain left, he settled a place separated from God and created an ungodly society. He actually built a city and named it after his son Enoch. (4:17). Matthew Henry made a comment that when Cain went out, he built this city with the intentions of never returning. He kept his mind busy building to drowned out his own sorrows and misery he was feeling for what he had done and now suffering. This describes Cain getting married and building this city. This had to have happened many years after his wondering was over and he settled. Other family members must have left the presence of the Lord to help settle this ungodly society.

CALEB

The Hebrew spelling of the name Caleb – כלב which is actually a compound word in Hebrew. Something that is quite common in ancient Hebrew. Col, Cuf + Lamed = all or whole. Lev, Lamed + Vet = heart. So, CALEB or COLEV as pronounced in Hebrew, actually means "whole hearted". Some will claim it means "dog", but that is the word Celeb, not Caleb. So, now that we have that covered, who was he? He was a faithful man of God found in the book of Numbers. He lived from 1484 to 1384 BC. He represented the tribe of Judah when Moses was choosing people to scout out the land before entering. This was the Land of Canaan that God had promised them. Caleb, along with Joshua, felt they should take it now while they had the chance and ten of the other spies told Moses no because they were afraid according to Numbers 13:30. Caleb was ignored by the people and so the Israelites wondered in the wilderness for forty years. When that generation died out, Caleb was 85 and believe it or not, he was as strong as ever and went to war against and drove out the three Anakites— Sheshai, Ahiman and Talmai, the sons of Anak. He also marched against the people living in Debir. This story shows us when we ignore the Lord, we suffer. What amazes me is the Lord still kept His promise. Caleb, along with Joshua was the one's that led the battle at their old age.

CYRUS

The name Cyrus comes from the Greek word Κυρος - Kyros, the Greek form of the Persian name Kūrush, which may mean "far sighted" or "young". The name is also associated with the Greek word κυριος - kyrios meaning "Lord". Cyrus was also known as Cyrus the Great. He was born between 590-580 BC and died around 529 BC. He is mentioned in the Bible over 20 times. He was king in Persia between 559-529 BC and he built his first empire by first conquering the Median Empire then the Lydian Empire, and eventually the Neo-Babylonian Empire. He was a pagan king but he was important to the Jewish history because he was the one responsible for the Jews returning to Israel after 70 years in captivity which was a prophecy by Jeremiah. Isaiah had predicted 150 years before Cyrus was even born that the temple would be rebuilt. Why this is so amazing is, Isaiah actually called him by name according to Isaiah 45:1,4. He helped them rebuild the temple in Jerusalem under Zerubbabel and Joshua the high priest. From 1879 to 1882 there were excavations dug in Babylon and they found a clay barrel that they now call the Cyrus Cylinder, which held a document that states Cyrus policies that went like this: "All of their peoples I gathered together and restored to their dwelling-places". This archology find is amongst many others that are continually proving the Bible accurate.

DANIEL

The name Daniel is from the Hebrew name דָּנִיֵּאל Daniyyel meaning God is my judge, from the roots דִּין din meaning "to judge" and אֵל el meaning "God". Daniel was a man of God and lived between 620—538 BC. When he was about 14, Jerusalem came under control of Nebuchadnezzar and he was taken captivity. They changed his name to Belteshazzar in Daniel 1:6-7, most likely to erase any connection to his Hebrew heritage. Daniel could also understand dreams (1:17). The book of Daniel was written in two different languages. In Hebrew and most of Chapter 2 and all of 3-7 was written in Aramaic. This was because most of the book was written for the Jews, but a portion was written for diplomacy so some of it was written in Aramaic. Daniel served under four different kings. Nebuchadnezzar, Belshazzar, Darius and Cyrus which he left Babylon after the first year of Cyrus in (1:21) Fun fact I didn't know, Daniel was actually in his 80's when he was thrown in the Lion's den. He always looked so young in the children's books. We know this because Darius was king at the time and he became king in 538 BC and Daniel died between 535 and 530 BC. This would have made him between 85 and 90 years old. So, Daniel was an old man in the den. If it was me, I would have figured God was done and that was the way I would be seeing my end. Not so fast, God had other plans.

DAVID

The name David is from the Hebrew name דָּוִד– Dawid, which was derived from Hebrew דּוֹד (dod) meaning Beloved or Uncle. David was one of the most talked about charters in the Old Testament. David was born around 1040 BC in Bethlehem. According to 2 Samuel 5:4-5; "David was thirty years old when he began to reign, and he reigned forty years. He reigned in Hebron for seven years and in Jerusalem he reigned thirty-three years. Commentaries state he was 70 when he died. In verse 5, his career is laid out. David was a young shepherd and upcoming musician. He defeated Goliath when he fought him with his sling in 1 Sam 17. Why did he pick up five stones? Because his training told him to. It had nothing to do with the lack of faith. What if the Philistines decided to attack him? He was prepared. King David wasn't perfect. He committed adultery with Bathsheba in 2 Sam 11 and he tried to cover it up by bring her husband Uriah home from the war to sleep with her. When that didn't work, he had him killed by sending him to the front lines without any backup. Then Nathan the prophet in 2 Sam 12, who was a close friend and adviser to him, came and confronted David by telling him a story. After David realized it, Nathan told him his son would die and he did. David repented in Psalm 51 and God gave them a son named Solomon.

DEBORAH

The name Deborah comes from the Hebrew name דְּבוֹרָה Devorah meaning Bee. I see her as Queen Bee because of what she accomplished as a woman in the Old Testament. She was married. The best I could find for when she lived was from 1107 BC to 1067 BC. So, who was she? She was one of the most influential women in the Bible. She was known for her wisdom. She was a prophet, judge, (the only woman judge and this word "judge" in the Hebrew is "Shofet" which means deliverer) warrior, poet and a singer as well as a songwriter. There was only one other person in the Bible that was a prophet and judge and that was Samuel. She was the ruler of the Hebrews in the Old Testament. She judged and led Israel for 20 years in the 12th century BC. When you read the book of Judges, you see people falling away from God, suffering for it and then coming back to God and repenting. For 20 years, she dealt with war with the Canaanites and then peace for 40 years thereafter according to Judges 5:31. When I was reading about her being judge, I didn't get the feeling she had any problems from anyone because she was a woman. She had the hand of God on her and she was respected as such. The Israelites believed in her abilities to rule and judge rightly. Judges 4:4-5 *"4 Now Deborah, a prophetess, the wife of Lapidoth, was judging Israel at that time. 5 And she would sit under the palm tree of Deborah between Ramah and Bethel in the mountains of Ephraim. And the children of Israel came up to her for judgment."*

ELI

The name Eli, עֵלִי, means "ascension" in Hebrew. He became judge when he was 58 years old and ruled for 40 years according to 1 Sam 4:18. He was 98 years old when died by falling back in his chair and breaking his neck. He was a Jewish priest living in the time of the Judges and serving God near the hill country of Ephraim. He had two wicked sons', Hophni and Phinehas, that were corrupt by working in the temple and stealing the good meat that was meant for sacrifice. They were also having sex with the girls that were at the doorway of the tent of meeting. (1 Sam 2:22) When Eli found out, he jumps their cases about it but did nothing. So, God sent a messenger to warn him that both sons would die the same day. (1 Sam 2:34) They both died by the Philistines hand when the Israelites fought them and lost 30,000 soldiers. This was the same time when the Ark of God was captured. (1 Sam 4:10-11) So, God kept His promise and raised up a new priest named Samuel through Eli. Samuel's mother couldn't have children and when she prayed about it in Eli's presence, Eli blessed her and told her she would have a son. When she did, she named him Samuel and gave him to the service of the Lord when he was weaned, which means he was between 2 –4 years old in those days. Samuel lived in the temple in the care of Eli. (1 Sam 1:24-28)

ELIJAH

The name Elijah comes from the Hebrew name אֵלִיָּהוּ Eliyyahu meaning "my God is YAHWEH", derived from the elements אֵל 'el and יָה (yah), both referring to the Hebrew God. Elijah was born around 900 BC in the village of Tishbe in Gilead. When did Elijah die? He didn't. In 2 Kings 2:11 the Lord took Elijah in a whirlwind up to Heaven. He was a prophet of God. He challenges Ahab in 1 Kings 17:1, an evil king that ruled over the northern kingdom from 874 BC to 853 BC. Elijah prophesies that a drought would come because of the evil that Ahab had done according to 1 Kings 17:1-7. God told Elijah to go and hide by a brook of Cherith and the ravens would feed him. Why a raven, because they are very resourceful in nature. We call them scavenger birds. As time goes on and the drought and famine got worse, he goes to Zarephath and lives there because God told him a widow would provide for him. She helps Elijah out by feeding him all she had and because of this, her flour bins and the jar of oil never runs dry until the rains came according to 1 Kings 17:8-16. Then from 18:17-40 he defeats the false prophets of Baal on Mount Carmel by calling down fire from Heaven when they couldn't. Awesome display of what God can do. Once he defeated them, God allowed rain to fall again 41-46. There is so much more to this story but bottom line, He was a delight in God's eyes. So much so, he escaped death.

ELISHA

The name Elisha comes from the Hebrew name אֱלִישָׁע' Elisha', a contracted form of אֱלִישׁוּעַ lishu'a meaning "my God is salvation". We don't know exactly when Elisha was born but we do know he lived the last half of the 9th century BC because he lived during the time of the kings, Joram king of Judah (851-843 BC), Jehu (843-814BC), Jehoahaz (814-798BC), and Joash king of Judah (835-796BC). He was a prophet according to 1 Kings 19:16 and a miracle worker. He was considered a biblical hero. He was the son of a rich farmer in Galilee. He was approached by Elijah while he was tilling in the family field according to 1 Kings 19:19. Elisha was involved in politics by helping kings' forces attack Moab and defend Israel against Syrian attacks. He was well liked among the leaders but, even though he was a disciple of Elijah, Elijah was always having issues with the kings and leaders. He met a Shunammite woman who was wealthy and her husband built an upper room for him to stay in when he was traveling. Elisha wanted to give her something because she was amazing to him. She had no children so he blessed her by saying this time next year you will have a son. She had a son a year later. When he was a bit older, he died and Elisha came and raised him from the dead in 2 kings 4:8-37. It's a good read. Even dead, Elisha's bones raised a man from the dead. 2 Kings 13:20-21. What an amazing God we serve.

ENOCH

The name Enoch is the Hebrew name חֲנוֹךְ Chanokh meaning "dedicated". Enoch was born to his father Jared around 3332 BC. He was also the father of Methuselah which at the time of his birth, Enoch was 65. He did not die but he was taken by God in 2967 BC at the age of 300 according to Genesis 5:22-24. Jared was 162 years old when Enock was born. To just be clear, there are four men named Enoch in the Bible but the one we are talking about is this one born of Jared. You can read more about him in Genesis 5:18. If you read in Hebrews 11:5, it is also mentioned that Enoch was taken up by God and did not experience death. There are only two people mentioned in the Bible that did not experience death and that is Elijah, which we already studied about and Enoch. The reason why God does this is because he continued to walk faithfully with God all his life. Another reason that many believe is so both him and Elijah would come back as the two witnesses that are mentioned in Revelation 11:3-12. This would make perfect since. I wanted to point out that in Jude 1:14, it says that Enoch was the seventh from Adam. People have mistaken this as Enoch being the seventh child of Adam but this isn't the case. He was seven generations down the line from Adam. Others will say this was Cain's son mentioned in Genesis 4:17 which doesn't fit with the time line.

Esau

The name Esau comes from the Hebrew name עֵשָׂו' Esaw which meant "hairy". He was a twin and was born to Rebekah and Isaac around 1836 BC. His twin brother was Jacob which they fought in the womb. Not much is said as to when Esau dies, but Esau was the older brother and he was the head of the Nation of Edom or Edomites which was a wicked nation. Esau was a hunter and very hairy. In Gen 25:27, his father loved him best. His mother loved Jacob the best. One day he had hunted all day and must have struck out because he claims he was about to die of starvation. In vs 29-34 Jacob told him he could have some of his food if he gave up his birthright, which meant a double portion of all the family inheritance. Esau did it. He ate himself out of house and home. Esau also got ripped off by Jacob by cheating him again from getting the Patriarchal blessings 27:14-16. Then Jacob took off because Esau vowed to kill Jacob. What can we understand about Esau? Esau had his sights set on the things of this world rather than God. He is the example of godless actions in the book of Hebrews 12:16-17. For the fact that he sold his birthright for one meal. The prophesy was foretold in Gen 25:23, Romans 9:12 that the older would serve the young between the two nations and it came true. God tells Malachi in 1:2-3 that He loved Jacob but hated Esau because of his wicked ways. Jacob wasn't perfect either as we will find out.

ESTHER

The name Esther was the name given to her by non-Jews which is אֶסְתֵּר in the Hebrew and Εσθηρ in the Greek which means "star" and it also could have come from the name of the Near Eastern goddess ISHTAR. In 2:7 her birth name is Hadassah which is Hebrew הֲדַס hadas meaning "myrtle tree" which is a sweet-smelling bitter tasting and sometimes a symbol for the righteous. I usually like to put in each writing when each person was born and where they were born. When they died and where they died but sometimes there is no answer. I can't find any solid evidence of when she was born but based on her husband, king Xerxes history, she was about 15 when she married him in 479 BC according to the Greek historian Herodotus. So, with this, she was born around 494 BC. Her father Abihail had died shortly after she was conceived and then her mother after she was born. Mordecai stepped in as the first cousin and raised her as his daughter. Abihail was Mordecai's blood uncle according to Esther 2:7. I don't have room to tell you the full story but Esther saves the Jews from being killed and the guy, Haman, that plotted against the Jews, was hung from the same gallows that he built for Mordecai to hang on. This was a cool biblical murder plot that went wrong and back fired on Haman. We see movies like this all the time and the good guy wins. Read it slowly or you might miss something.

EVE

The name Eve comes from the Hebrew name חַוָּה Chawwah, which was derived from the Hebrew word חָוָה chawah meaning "to breathe" or the related word חָיָה chayah meaning "to live". Eve was not born; she was created out of the rib of Adam around 4004 BC in the Garden of Eden. She is called Eve because she is the mother of all living according to Genesis 3:20. Eve had two deaths. She experienced a spiritual death when her and Adam sinned against God, none like anyone has ever known since. One day they are walking with God the Son and having one on one fellowship with Him and the next, they are separated from Him because they allowed sin into the Garden and their lives. The second death was a physical death which the Bible doesn't say anything about when she died but she probably died around the same time Adam did. We know that Eve's choice to sin caused all women after her, as well as herself, to received two curses. The first one we read about in Genesis 3:16 is intense pain in giving birth. Even after 6000 years, with all the medical advancements, we have not been able to take away all the pain that comes with child bearing. The second is that she would have different ideas then Adam, even confrontations but ultimately, he is in charge and is ruler over her. Some men take this part way too far. As a man, I'm telling all men to memorize Ephesians 5:25.

EZEKIEL

The name Ezekiel comes from the Hebrew name יְחֶזְקֵאל Yechezqel meaning "God will strengthen", from the roots חָזַק chazaq meaning "to strengthen" and אֵל׳ el meaning "God". Ezekiel was born in Jerusalem around 622 BC and the closes anyone can figure is he died around 569 BC in Babylon. He was the author of the Book of Ezekiel. He wrote it around 565 BC. He was a priest in the temple and was also taken captive to Babylon when he was 25. When he was there, he was called to be a prophet of God at the age of 30. He was the fourth of five major prophets in the Old Testament. As a prophet in the Old Testament, you were usually warning people about their coming destruction. He did this by using prophecies, signs, parables and symbols. When I have warned people, they take it as being judged, which the word judge or judging comes from the Greek word "Krino" which means "To call into question". We all do that all the time. We have to in order to protect ourselves and others, if they will listen. Ezekiel was told by God if he did not deliver the warnings of the punishment to come, then Ezekiel would be held accountable for their blood. The Bible tells us that Ezekiel had no issues with delivering God's message. As you can imagen, he wasn't well received by everyone he spoke to, but he knew this. He truly didn't want people to die, but to listen and turn back to God.

Ezra

The name Ezra in the Hebrew is עֶזְרָא which means "help". He was born in Babylon in 480 BC and died 440 BC. He is the author of the book of Ezra which was written between 457 and 444 BC. During chapters 6-7 is when Esther lives and rules in Persia. This is a period of about 60 years. He was a scribe and a priest according to Ezra 7:11. He was a godly man and is seen by God as a strong trusted man in God with moral integrity and a victor over sin. He was living in Babylon during the seventh year of the reign of king Artaxerxes, the king of Persia in 457 BC. Ezra shows how God fulfills his promise in all of Ch 1 of letting his people go back to Judea. Interesting fact, out of approximately 3 million people that were in captivity, less than 50,000 people returned. This was considered the second Exodus. Most wonder why they all don't leave. After 70 years, would you want to leave if you are used to living a certain way? It took about 4 months for these people to travel 900 miles which I'm surprised it wasn't longer considering the territory they had to cover. There were only three tribes that returned. Judah, Benjamin and Levi. When they rebuilt the Temple, it took 21 years after the foundations were built because there was a 14-year break. It was opposed because of the fear of no taxes would be paid. (4:13). Work resumed 520 BC and 515 BC it was completed.

GIDEON

The name Gideon is the Hebrew גִּדְעוֹן name that means "feller, hewer". He lived from 1252 to 1152 BC and he was the 5th Judge according to Judges 6:11-8:32. Out of all 12 Judges, even though he is very humble, he is known as the greatest judge of Israel. Gideon is the one we read about in Sunday School who tested God by putting out the fleece in 6:37-39 to make sure he hears God correctly about saving the Israelite people. Gideon does what Deut 6:16 says not to but he seems to do this a lot. First, he requires God to put dew on a fleece he lays out, instead of on the ground. Then, he asks for the opposite, a dry fleece and wet ground. Then, once more, the opposite. With just 300 men to fight the Midianites, Gideon and his Army never even raise a hand to them, they just make a lot of noise, this confuses the men in the Midianite camp, and they end up killing each other in the chaos. What else do we know about Gideon? We see 9 traits in him, which they weren't all good. We see humility which was pleasing to the Lord. He showed caution by testing what he thought he heard from the Lord. He had a strong spirituality. He had divine inspiration and a divine fellowship. By the way he planned out his attack, you could tell he was strategic minded. He had tact when he spoke to the Lord. He was very loyal to God, but his biggest weakness was he was weakened by prosperity. Eight out of nine isn't bad.

HAGAR

The name Hagar is the Hebrew word הָגָר which means "flight". She lived from 1930 BC to 1840 BC. She was actually Egyptian so the word could be from an unknown Egyptian origin. She was a slave to Abram's wife, Sarai (KJV). In Genesis 16, Hagar is basically made to be a surrogate mother because Abram and Sarai are impatient with God after waiting 10 years and still no children. When Hagar started to show, Sarai got jealous because she was young and probably beautiful and started treating her very badly. This caused Hagar to run away into the wilderness according to verse 5-7. She was met by an angle that told her to go back and the Lord would give her a big family line. She had a son named Ishmael and he wouldn't be liked by many. Fast forward 14 years when Isaac was born. A little time had passed after Isaac had been weaned when Ishmael had been bullying Isaac 21:8-9. Sarai saw this and told Abram to "Cast out" Hagar and Ishmael. They went into the wilderness and when they had no food or water, she put him under a bush to die and the angle of the Lord made her a promise that out of Ishmael would be a great nation and he provided a well of water Genesis 21:16-20. Because of Abrams sin with Hagar, the people of Isaac, which were the Jews and the people of Ishmael which were the Arabs, hated each other and there was war between the two peoples which resulted in much bloodshed.

HANNAH

The name Hannah comes from the Hebrew word חַנָּה Channah
meaning "favor, grace", derived from the root חָנַן chanan. She lived
during the period of the Judges, which her son Samuel was the last
Judge. (1 Sam 12). Hannah was one of two wives' of Elkanah.
Peninnah was the other wife. They lived in the hill country of
Ephraim which is north of Judah. To start out this story, Hannah
had no children and Peninnah did according to 1 Sam 1:2. It was
a disgrace to be barren in those days. Often times the wife that did
have children was loved more. Not Elkanah. He loved Hannah
very much and he would give her double portions when they would
go make an offering each year in the city. The scripture goes on to
say in verses 6-7 that Peninnah would make mean remarks to
Hannah about not being able to have children. Through this,
Hannah would respond in grace. She would restrain from saying
anything back to Peninnah that was unkind. Hannah finally called
out to God and in verse 20, Hannah conceived and had Samuel.
She promised God He could have Samuel once he was old enough
and she kept her promise. He went to live with Eli the priest at the
tabernacle to serve the Lord. God's blessings did not end. Hannah
had 5 more children according to 1 Sam 2:21.

HEZEKIAH

The name Hezekiah comes from the Hebrew name is חִזְקִיָּהוּ Chizqiyahu, which means "YAHWEH strengthens", from the roots חָזַק chazaq meaning "to strength" and יָה yah referring to the Hebrew God. He was born 740 BC and he was 25 years old (2 Kings 18:1-3) when he became the 13th king of Judah and he reigned for 29 years from 715 — 686 BC. He was only 54 years old when he died. He was considered a good king in God's eyes. 2 Chronicles 31:20 says he did what was good, right and true before the Lord. The scripture goes on to say he did it with all his heart. Because of this, he is mentioned in many places in the old testament. His story is repeated in 2 Kings 16:20—20:21; 2 Chronicles 28:27—32:33; and Isaiah 36:1—39:8. He is also mentioned in Proverbs 25:1; Isaiah 1:1; Jeremiah 15:4; 26:18–19; Hosea 1:1; and Micah 1:1. Hezekiah came from a wicked father by the name of king Ahaz. Most of the time when the father is wicked, it is passed down but when Hezekiah became king, he cleaned house. Ahaz's father, king Jotham, was a godly king in 2 Chronicles 27:2 so it is a wonder why Ahaz left the teachings of the Lord. Hezekiah had a strong zeal for the Lord so much that he destroyed the pagan altars, idols, and temples and even the bronze serpent that Moses made in Numbers 21:9. He cleaned out the temple in Jerusalem that his father closed up and reopened it. He is worth reading more about.

HOSEA

The name Hosea is the Hebrew word הוֹשֵׁעַ; Hoshea, which mean "salvation". He was born in the 8th century BC to his father Beeri and was active between the years of 750—722. He was one of the minor prophets of the Old Testament. Hosea is considered the prophet of doom. He is told by God to actually marry a prostitute which he did by the name of Gomer, because the land has committed great harlotry by departing from the Lord. (1:2). This is a perfect example of God loving us. He won't fail us, but we will him. They had three children together. A son named Jezreel, which means "God sows", after the Valley of Jezreel. A daughter named Lo-ruhamah which means "not loved" in Hebrew who was renamed Ruhamah meaning "loved". Her name change represents "that God will first withdraw His 'loving mercy' and at last restore it." They had a third son named Lo-Ammi which meant "not many people". God was extremely upset with Israel because they had left Him to live in sexual sin among other things. He promises in time that he will restore them in Hosea 2:14-23. Through the story, Gomer is unfaithful to Hosea and leaves him for other men in 3:1-5. God uses this to show Israel that they have done the same thing to Him. God wants to restore His people but He has no problem chastising them either. He sends people our way like Hosea to warn us.

ISAAC

The name Isaac comes from the Hebrew name יִצְחָק Yitzchaq meaning "he will laugh, he will rejoice", derived from צָחַק tzachaq meaning "to laugh". This is because God told Abraham and his wife they were going to have a baby and they laughed. He was 100 years old according to Gen 21:5 and Sarah was 90. There are different ideas of when Isaac was born but most believe he was born 1896 BC in Canaan and died 1716 BC. He lived 180 years according to Gen 35:28. Isaac was the second son of Abraham. His first son was Ishmael. We all know the story of his father obeying God by taking him up on the mountain to sacrifice him and God stopped him Gen 22:1-14. Did you know that he married his cousin Rebekah Gen 24:15? It's weird to think of that, but Abraham didn't want him to marry a Canaanite wife according to Gen 24:3. So, Abraham's servant prayed and God directed him to her. Isaac was 60 years old when he had twin son's named Esau and Jacob according to Gen 25:26. He loved Esau more than he did Jacob and Rebekah favored Jacob. When Isaac was 75, his father Abraham died and left him everything according to Gen 25:5. In verse 9 it says that Isaac and Ishmael buried their father together. So even though the two nations did not get along, they came together on this one. Esau and Jacob did the same thing when Isaac died. Gen 35:27 states they were in Hebron when he died which is 18 miles south of Jerusalem.

ISAIAH

The name Isaiah comes from the Hebrew name יְשַׁעְיָהוּ Yesha'yahu meaning "YAHWEH is salvation", from the roots יָשַׁע yasha' meaning "to save" and יָהּ yah referring to the Hebrew God. He is the author of the Book of Isaiah. He was born in Jerusalem in the 8th century to Amoz according to Isa 1:1. He was married and had sons of his own. One named Shear-Jashub which means "the remnant shall return" and Maher-shalal-hash-baz which means "speed the spoil and hasten the booty". Both of these names contained messages from God to Judah's king, king Ahaz according to Isa 8:1-4. He was considered to be one of the greatest prophets in the Bible and he was a priest. He received his calling in the temple according to Isa 6:4. This was a place where only priest could go so it stands to reason he was a priest. His prophesies were directed towards mostly Judah and Israel but to other nations as well. He is known as the prophet of Judah or as some people would say, Judah's evangelist because he worked extremely hard to get Judah back to God. He believed that Judah was God's chosen according Isa 43:10. He wrote many prophesies down including the birth of Christ in Isa 9:6. Then he prophesied about the torture and death of Jesus in Ch 53. In 65:17-25 Isaiah predicts the new heavens and new earth just like John saw in his visions when he was imprisoned on the island of Patmos in Revelation 21.

ISHMAEL

The name Ishmael comes from the Hebrew name יִשְׁמָעֵאל Yishma'el meaning "God will hear", from the roots שָׁמַע shama' meaning "to hear" and אֵל 'el meaning "God". Ishmael was born, according to my Bible timeline, 1910 BC to Abraham and his wife's slave Hagar. He was Abraham's first son and because he was conceived in sin, many problems came after. God had already promised a son with Sarah. The Lord told Hagar that Ishmael would be a wild man and no one would like him nor would he like anyone. After Isaac came along and was a small child, Ishmael tormented Isaac and they were sent away to die. Through all the troubles that Ishmael caused and went through, God still promised him that he would become a nation according to Genesis 21:17-19. When he grew into a man, he lived in the desert and became an archer. His mother found him a wife in Egypt according to verse 20-21. This could have been because she was Egyptian. I couldn't find much about his wife but a few commentaries stated he had two wives. One he divorced and the second he had all these children with. Whoever the mother or mothers were, we know that these were his children according to Genesis 25:12-15. Starting from the oldest; Nebajoth, Kedar, Adbeel, Mibsam, Mishma, Dumah, Massa, Hadar, Tema, Jetur, Naphish, and Kedemah. Great bloodshed came from this family.

JACOB

The name Jacob comes from the Latin word Iacobus, which was from the Greek Ιακωβος Iakobos, which was from the Hebrew name יַעֲקֹב Ya'aqov. He is the son of Isaac and Rebekah and was born around 1836 BC and died around 1689 BC. He was the youngest twin. His twin brother was Esau. Jacob was the leader of the nation of Israel. The twelve tribes of Israel came from him. The scripture says while Esau enjoyed hunting, Jacob liked to stick around the tents in verse Gen 25:27. He had a rough start. He conned his brother Esau out of his birth right in verses 29-34. Esau had the choice but Jacob could have shared. He also stole his brothers blessing by deceiving his father Isaac. 27:1-40. Isaac was old, blind and near death according to 27:2-4, or so he thought, when all this happened. Jacob left and settled in Haran and worked for his uncle Laban. He loved his cousin Rachel and made a deal to work for his uncle seven years for Rachel. Jacob found out what comes around goes around. Laban deceived him and gave him Leah. He had to work another seven years for Rachel. He kept both wife's but loved Rachel more. Guess who could have children and who couldn't. You guessed it. Leah could have children and Rachel couldn't at first. God did open Rachel's womb in 30:22-24 and she bore Joseph. Altogether, Jacob had 13 children. All boys except for a daughter Dinah which was Leah's last child. Rachel only had two and she died with the last one which was Benjamin.

JEREMIAH

The name Jeremiah comes from the Hebrew name יִרְמְיָהוּ Yirmiyahu meaning "YAHWEH will exalt", from the roots רום (rum) meaning "to exalt" and יָה (yah) referring to the Hebrew God. He is the writer of the Book of Jeremiah and He is considered one of the major prophets of the Hebrew Bible or what we call the Old Testament. He was born to the priest Hilkiah in a small village called Anathoth (Jeremiah 1:1) around 643 BC. The village was about 3 miles northeast from Jerusalem. His family was known as a priestly family so it stands to reason the call to be a prophet was sure to come. I don't think he expected it between 13 to 16 years of age. His ministry lasted over 40 years. The reason it is believed he was a teenager is Josiah started his reign the same year Jeremiah was born. The thirteenth year of Josiah's reign was 627 BC. According to Jeremiah 1:2, this is when a word from the Lord came to Jeremiah, thus being a teenager. He also tells the Lord he is too young in 1:6. He was the prophet that God sent to Judah in their last days before God had cast them out of the land like He did with the 10 northern tribes that had ignored His warnings. They ignored Jeremiahs warnings in 44:16 and even said they would continue to worship their false gods. During this time, he was tortured for trying to warn them. God sent a word of destruction to them for their choice according to verses 26-29. Jeremiah died in Egypt in 570 BC.

JOB

The name Job comes from the Hebrew name אִיּוֹב 'Iyyov, which means "persecuted, hated". The author of the Book of Job is unknown, but scholars are leaning towards Moses. With doing extensive research, I found out that very little is known about when Job was born, but we do know he was born after the flood because he mentions it in Job 22:16. Some speculate between 2350 and 1750 BC which is just too much of a gap for me. His life span is speculated at 200 years. We know he lived long enough to raise two whole families. He lived in the land called Uz. If you have any Biblical knowledge, you know that Job lost his whole family because God allowed Satan to test him and Job being a righteous man, passed the test. During that time, his friends, Eilhu, Ephaz and Zophar visited him and believed Job had sinned in some way. They argued with Job about it. Job stood his ground and won. We know he was a rich man because in Job 1:3, we see that he had 7000 sheep, 3000 camels, 500 oxen, 500 female donkeys and a very large household, which means there would have been servants working for him and his very large family. He was allowed to be attacked to show that wealth was not a vice for Job. Once Job had proved his love for God, God restored to Job a whole new family and doubled the livestock he lost. Job 42:12-13 states that he lived another 140 years and saw four generations and died full of days.

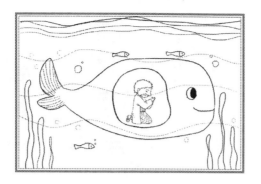

JONAH

The name Jonah came from the Hebrew name יוֹנָה Yonah meaning "dove". According to most scholars, Jonah was born in 800 BC and died 740 BC. According to 2 Kings 14:25 Jonah was born in Gath-Hepher, Israel. His father was Amittai. He is listed in the Old Testament as the 5th minor prophet. His name means dove, yet he was proud (not the good kind), stubborn, a complainer and was disobedient and the Bible doesn't say he ever got over himself. Jonah had a real issue with being prejudice. The people of Nineveh were vile nasty people that were pagan's and Jonah did not believe these people were worth saving. In fact, when God called Jonah to take a message to these people, Jonah disobeyed and left on a boat to go to Tarshish. He wanted to put as much space between him and Nineveh and that was the place to go because it was 2200 miles in the opposite direction. He hated the Assyrians, but God had chosen Jonah and He wasn't going to let Jonah get off that easy. We all know the story so, fast forward to chapter 3. Nineveh was so big; it would take three days to cross it on foot according to verse 3. As he walked, he cried out that they would be destroyed and they all believed. In chapter 4 Jonah was angry and would rather die than to see these people come to the Lord. The Lord tried to reason with him and he sat pouting about it. The chapter ends with no indication of Jonah ever accepted it.

JONATHAN

The name Jonathan comes from the Hebrew name יְהוֹנָתָן Yehonatan, contracted to יוֹנָתָן Yonatan, meaning "YAHWEH has given", derived from the roots יְהוֹ yeho referring to the Hebrew God and נָתַן natan meaning "to give". There are actually ten people named Jonathan in the Bible, but we are going to focus on king Saul's oldest son. He was born around 1095 BC. He was the best friend of David and had to make a hard choice. Betray his father or allow David to be killed. So, who was Jonathan? He was a man with integrity and a faithful man. He not only was David's friend; he was his brother-in-law. David married to Jonathan's sister Michal according to 1 Sam 18:20-21. King Saul hated David and had plotted to have him killed, but when Jonathan heard about it, he told David to hide in 1 Sam 19:1-2. In verses 3-7, Jonathan reminded his father of what David had done for him by killing the Philistine and how the Lord brought great deliverance for all Israel and how he rejoiced. Once Jonathan pointed this out, his father promised to not kill him according to verse 6. "So, Saul heeded the voice of Jonathan, and Saul swore, "As the Lord lives, he shall not be killed." As you can tell, Jonathan was nothing like his father. Jonathan had love beyond measure and was very loyal to his friends. He died during a battle with the Philistines along with his brothers Abinadab and Malchishua in 1 Sam 31.

JOSHUA

The name Joshua comes from the Hebrew name יְהוֹשֻׁעַ Yehoshu'a meaning "YAHWEH is salvation", from the roots יְהוֹ yeho referring to the Hebrew God and יָשַׁע yasha' meaning "to save". It is speculated Joshua was born around 1500 BC. We know he was born to Nun in Goshen which is in the lower part of Egypt prior to the Exodus. He would have been close to 40 when they left Egypt because when he and Caleb went to spy out the Promise Land, the scripture says that Caleb was 40 years old in Joshua 14:7. Many scholars believe that Joshua would have been close to the same age. He was Moses' second in command and he is the one that leads the people into the promise land after Moses died. Joshua was one of the best military leaders in history. He defeated the Amalekites with his sword, but with the help of Moses, Aaron and Hur. When Moses arms would drop, Amalek would start winning, when his arms were up, Israel would win. So, Aaron and Hur held his arms up and Joshua, along with his army, defeated Amalekites. Joshua had faith like Caleb, very solid. They both reported back to Moses that they could take the land despite what they saw. The other ten spies were afraid and told Moses that it was impossible. Because of this, they wondered in the wilderness for 40 years. When Joshua finally took the land, he was between 78 and 80 years old. He died at 110 years old according to Joshua 24:29.

JOSIAH

The name Josiah come from the Hebrew name יֹאשִׁיָהוּ Yoshiyahu meaning "YAHWEH supports". He was born around 648 BC and in 2 Kings 22:1 it explains that Josiah was 8 years old when he became king of Jerusalem and he reigned for 31 years. He was known as the world's youngest king. His mother's name was Jedidah. His father was king Amon and the grandson of king Manasseh, which both were evil kings that ruled over Judah. But Josiah was a righteous king before God. We know this because in 2 Kings 22:2 it states *"And he did what was right in the sight of the Lord, and walked in all the ways of his father David; he did not turn aside to the right hand or to the left."* From verses 3-7 it shows us that Josiah raised money to repair the temple. During this time, Hilkiah the High Priest, found the Book of the Law and read and gave it to Shaphan to read, then he read it to the king. Then Josiah called for a national repentance because of all the idol worship. They cleaned house. They took all of the idols and any pagan worship objects and destroyed them. Then Josiah restored the observance of the Passover according to 23:2-23. In verse 25 it says that there was no king like him who had turned to the Lord with all his heart and no one like him afterward. Josiah died in battle against the Egyptian Pharaoh Necho at Megiddo and he was buried in Jerusalem. His son Jehoahaz became king after that.

LEAH

The name Leah comes from the Hebrew name לֵאָה Le'ah, which was probably derived from the Hebrew word לְאָה le'ah meaning "weary". Her father's name was Laban and her younger sister was Rachel. She was the wife and cousin of Jacob. Jacob worked seven years for her younger sister Rachel and her father Laban tricked Jacob into marrying Leah. By rights, Leah should have been the first to be married because she was older. I feel sad for her because she only wanted to be loved by Jacob, but Jacob loved her sister Rachel more. The scripture doesn't say she was ugly like so many preachers preach, it just says in Genesis 29:17 *"Leah was tender eyed; but Rachel was beautiful and well favoured."* (KJV) Many commentators agree that this just means Rachel had a figure that was much better and she was like a beauty queen compared to Leah. The Lord had compassion on Leah in verse 31 and opened her womb. She had this idea if she kept boring him children, he would eventually love her. She gave him seven children. Six sons and one daughter. The names of her children were Reuben the firstborn, then Simeon, Levi, which became the father of the tribe of Levi. Then Judah, which became the father of the tribe of Judah. Issachar and Zebulun. Her daughter was Dinah. She was raped by Shechem and her brothers Simon and Levi killed him and every male in the city Genesis 34.

MELCHIZEDEK

The name Melchizedek is the Hebrew word מלכי-צדק that means "my king is righteous" from Hebrew מֶלֶךְ mélekh "king" and צֶדֶק tzédek "justice, righteousness". As odd as it may be for the Book of Genesis, there is no record of his birth or death. In Hebrews 7:3 it states, *"without father, without mother, without genealogy, having neither beginning of days nor end of life, but made like the Son of God, remains a priest continually."* His very name means "king of righteousness". He is mentioned in Genesis 14:18-20 as being priest of the Most High God. Psalms 110:4 *"You are a priest forever according to the order of Melchizedek.",* In Hebrews 6:20 it states that Jesus has become High Priest forever after the order of Melchizedek. There was an Aaronic priesthood which was hereditary. You had to be in the family line of Aaron to receive this but never the less, all you had to do is be family. They were also only priests of the nation of Israel. Then there was the Melchizedekian priesthood which is eternal or timeless and no other people are mentioned in the Bible of being in this priesthood other than Jesus. Some would speculate that Jesus and Melchizedek were the same person. Are they the same person? Well, Melchizedek is a type of Christ that is for sure. They both share the same eternal order that cannot be shared by anyone else and according to scriptural evidence, it would sure seem that way. If anyone claims to have either one of these priestly orders in todays world, he is a liar and would be considered to be involved in a cult.

METHUSELAH

The name Methuselah means "man of the dart" in Hebrew. According to my Bible timeline, he was born in 3317 BC and died 969 years later which would have been in 2348 BC, the same year as the Great Flood or close to it, depending on who you ask. He was the oldest person in recorded history. He was the son of Enoch, which was one of two people who did not experience death. In Genesis 5 it states he had a son named Lamech who was the father of Noah. It also states he had other sons and daughters but it doesn't say who they were. My Bible timeline shows that both Lamech and Methuselah were alive during the building of the Ark but died before the ark set sail. Some believe that Methuselah died a week before the flood because God had Noah go into the ark seven days before the waters came for a time of mourning. There are other places in the Bible that talk about a time of seven days of mourning such as, Genesis 50:3,7. Typically this was the standard. I couldn't find anything that stated they helped with the building of the ark, but there isn't anything that stated they didn't. The thing is, there wasn't much about his life stated in scripture. He was raised by Enoch which had God's favor so much so that he escaped death. This would have meant that he raised him to serve the Lord. I would have liked to know what Methuselah did for the Lord. What was his livelihood.

Miriam

The name Miriam is the Hebrew מִרְיָם form of Mary, which means bitterness or rebellion. She is recognized as "Miriam the prophetess in Exodus 15:20. She is the daughter of Amram and Jochebed, which as gross as it may be, Jochebed was Amram's father's sister according to Exodus 6:20. Miriam came from the tribe of Levi and the oldest of Moses and Aaron. It is believed she was about 10 to 12 years of age when she watched her baby brother Moses float down the Nile to the princess, which was Pharaoh's daughter. She was the one who also volunteered to take care of him when they needed a maid. She also volunteered her mother to nurse him and the princess agreed. Years later Miriam leads the women in song and dance when they escape the Egyptians in Ex 15:20-22. Later, Miriam complains about the actions of Moses marrying a Cushite woman and questions the Lord's wisdom in Numbers 12:1-2. The Lord gets angry and strikes her with leprosy and Moses asks God to forgive her and after seven days being outside the camp to heal, she was healed in Numbers 12:13-16. They couldn't travel anywhere because of what she did for a whole week. This is a good lesson. Don't be jealous of what the Lord has given other believers. Be happy with what the Lord has given you and give the Lord your best. Because of Miriam's disobedience, she was not allowed into the promise land. She died in Kadesh and was buried there. She was a mighty woman of God but had to pay for her disobedience.

MORDECAI

The name Mordecai is the Hebrew word מָרְדְּכַי means "servant of Marduk" in Persian. His birth is a mystery but a few scholars say he was born around 586 BC because he was captured by Nebuchadnezzar and taken to Babylon when Jerusalem was destroyed. This is when he was first mentioned in Esther 2:5-7. It explains that he was from the tribe of Benjamin. He was the older cousin to Ester, which he had taken care of because her father and mother had died. He was the son of Jair. He was very important to the safety of Esther and the Jewish people. He was the one that asked Esther to not reveal her Jewish background for her safety when she went up to the king's palace as one of the virgins to be looked at as the next queen to king Ahasuerus. According to Esther 2:21-23, one day Mordecai was sitting at the gate and overheard a plot to kill the king and told Esther about it. She reported it to the king and his name was recorded in the chronicles, not being rewarded at the time. He was later honored when the king couldn't sleep and had the chronicles read to him and he realized that Mordecai hadn't been rewarded. Haman, a guy that hated him the most because Mordecai wouldn't bow down to him, had to parade him around the streets. Haman had a plot to kill all Jews in order to see Mordecai die and once it was discovered in Esther 7:1-10, the king had Haman hung. Mordecai in turn, became second to the king.

MOSES

The name Moses is from the Hebrew name מֹשֶׁה Mosheh, which most people likely believe it derived from the Egyptian meaning "son", but could also possibly mean "deliver" in Hebrew. He is one of the most important people in the Bible, in fact, he writes the first five books of the Bible under the direction of God Himself. When he was a baby, he was spared because his mother put him in a basket and sent him down the river. Then Pharaoh's daughter finds him, his mother and sister end up raising him. His parents were Amram and Jockebed and as far as when he was born, no one can agree on a date but my Bible time line says around 1572 BC. He had an older sister named Miriam and an older brother name Aaron. Moses is responsible, along with his brother Aaron, for bring the children of Israel out of Egypt despite he had a speech impediment. But like so many leaders, they messed up and didn't get to go into the promise land. He sent 12 spies to spy out the promise land and 10 of them said it was a bad idea to go take the land and since Moses listened to the majority, they wonder 40 years in the wilderness. Many things happened during that time. According to Deut 34:5-7 Moses died in Moab and he was 120 years old. Unlike most people in the Bible, there is so much information about Moses. But, since he wrote the first five books of the Bible, that makes perfect since.

NAAMAN

The name Naaman is the Hebrew word נַעֲמָן meaning of the boy's name Naaman is "pleasant; pleasantness" or even "beautiful; agreeable; delightful." Although the Bible doesn't give a detailed account of when he was born, we know that he lived during the same time Elisha did because Elisha healed him of Leprosy according to 2 Kings 5. This would have been between 870 and 840 BC. He was the commander of the army of the king of Syria and was great and honorable in the eyes of his master however, he was a leper according to 2 Kings 5:1. The story starts off talking about a young girl that the Syrian army had captured from Israel. She was now a servant to Naaman's wife and she had an idea and told her if Naaman would go see the prophet who was in Samaria, he would heal him of leprosy. So Naaman went to Israel with a letter to the king of Israel taking gifts of money and clothing. When the king of Israel read it, he tore his clothes and asked if he was God. Elisha got involved and told Naaman to go wash in the Jordan seven times and he would be clean. Naaman got mad and went away. His servants told him to do what Elisha told him if he wanted to be healed in verse 13. Once he did, he was healed. He went to Elisha to pay him, but Elisha wouldn't take it. He asked if the Lord would forgive him when he took his master into the temple to worship Rimmon, a false god and Elisha assured him God would be with him verse 19.

Naomi

The name Naomi is from the Hebrew name נָעֳמִי Na'omi meaning "pleasantness". She was born around 1320 BC and she was the wife of Elimelech. She lived in Bethlehem with her two sons Mahlon and Kilion. When the famine came, according to Ruth 1:1, they moved to Moab for 10 years in 1294 BC. Then her sons married women from the area named Orpah and Ruth. Then in Ruth 1:3-5, her husband and both sons die. Later, Naomi hears that the famine is over and moves back home but only Ruth goes with her. Naomi tells both daughters they can stay with their people but Ruth loves Naomi and goes with her. Naomi name means pleasantness which leads us to think she was a wonderful person and a very lovely person. So much so that Ruth is willing to leave her own people to take care of Naomi the rest of her days. Naomi helps to play match maker when Ruth meets Boaz. She encourages Ruth to go to Boaz when he sleeps on the threshing floor according to Ruth 3:4. She wants to make sure Ruth would have a future and Boaz would provide that future since he was a wealth man. It wasn't hard to match them up because Boaz had asked about her and told her to not glean in any other field then his in 2:5, 8-9. Naomi was blessed in the end because she gained a son-in-law and 7 grandchildren through Ruth. Boaz took care of both Naomi and Ruth. God blessed Naomi for her faithfulness.

NEBUCHADNEZZAR

The name Nebuchadnezzar is from בוּכַדְנֶאצַּר Nevukhadnetzzar, the Hebrew form of the Akkadian name Nabu-kudurri-usur meaning "Nabu protect my eldest son", derived from the god's name NABU combined with kudurru meaning "eldest son" and an imperative form of naṣāru meaning "to protect". He was born around 634 BC to his father Nabopolassar and around 604 to 605 BC, took over as king of Babylon. He was considered the Bible's greatest villain. He destroyed both Judah and Jerusalem in 586 BC. Without knowing it, he served God in bring judgement on Judah for turning their back on God with their idol worship according to Jeremiah 25:9 *"and Nebuchadnezzar the king of Babylon, My servant,"* which he didn't serve God willingly, God was just allowing him to destroy Judea. Later though, God gave him a dream and he wanted it interpreted but none of his astrologers or wise man could do it so he had them killed. Daniel was able to and Nebuchadnezzar announced that his God was the God of gods according to Daniel 2:47. He didn't worship God though because we see in Daniel 3, he wanted Shadrach, Meshach and Abednego to worship his golden statue. When God protected those three, again, he claimed their God was truly God 3:28-29. He still didn't get it until Daniel Ch 4:3, 34-37. These verses would lead one to think that he turned to God in the end.

NEHEMIAH

The name Nehemiah is the Hebrew word נְחֶמְיָה which means 'Yahweh comfort" in Hebrew, derived from נָחַם nacham meaning "to comfort" and יָה yah referring to the Hebrew God. His father was Hachaliah. I didn't find anything about his mother. He was born around 480 BC like Ezra was. He is the writer of the book of Nehemiah and he starts his story off with asking king Artaxerxes if he can go to Jerusalem to start rebuild Jerusalem's walls. He gave him permission and he left. When he got there and started building in 2:19-20, Sanballat the Horonite, Tobiah the Ammonite official, and Geshem the Arab laughed when they heard about it. He defended himself by saying "*The God of heaven Himself will prosper us; therefore, we His servants will arise and build, but you have no heritage or right or memorial in Jerusalem.*" There were many people involved in the project. In Ch 4, their enemies plotted to go against them, but God protected them. Nehemiah had half his people guard while the others worked. They worked hard and had to deal with persecution. The wall was completed in Chapter 7 and they set up the temple staff. In Chapter 8, Ezra the priest brought the Book of The Revelation of Moses that God had commanded for Israel and read from it facing the town. He reads from it from chapter 8 –13. As you can see, Nehemiah was a prayer warrior. He kept his faith strong, even when faced with death.

NOAH

The name Noah comes from the Hebrew name נֹחַ Noach meaning "rest, repose", derived from the root נוּחַ nuach. He was a very obedient man of God. His father was Lamech and his grandfather was Methuselah. He was born, according to my Bible timeline, 2950 BC. He lived 950 years and he was directed by God to build an ark. Once he started, it took him 120 years. Noah is recognized as a preacher in 2 Peter 2:5. You can bet he told people what he was doing and as you can see, only his family believed him. He didn't start having children until he was 500 according to Genesis 5:32. He had three sons. Japheth, which is the oldest according to Gen 10:21. Then he had Shem and then Ham, which was the youngest according to Gen 9:22-24. The Bible states he had daughters as well. When he was 600 according to Gen 7:6, Noah and his family entered the ark, which was 450 feet long. If you compare it to the Titanic which was 850 feet long, you can see it wasn't very big to carry all those animals and his family. According to Gen 7:2-3 it states that Noah took in SEVEN, not TWO of every clean animal along with the birds and TWO of every unclean animal. Sunday school teachers teach that wrong a lot. It did rain for 40 days and nights according to verse 12, but they were actually in the ark for over 370 days. Add it up starting with Gen 7:11, 8:13-14. The Bible states the ark rested on Mount Ararat in Turkey, but no one has yet to find it. Jesus references Noah in Matt 24:37-39 as to His coming.

RACHEL

The name Rachel is the Hebrew word name רָחֵל Rachel meaning "ewe". She was the daughter of Laban and a cousin to Jacob and Esau. She was born around 1800 BC according to my Bible timeline and lived in Harran, where she met Jacob her husband. She had an older sister named Leah, which became Jacob's wife first through trickery. She had two children with Jacob named Joseph and Ben-Oni, which she died having Ben-Oni. Later his name was changed to Benjamin. The story takes place in Genesis 29 when she meets Jacob and he falls in love. He makes a deal with his uncle to work seven years for him and in exchange, he is allowed to marry her. When that time was up, he's tricked into marrying the older sister Leah. In those days, it was customary for the older daughter to be married off first. So then, because he loved Rachel more, he worked another seven years for her. When they get married, she was found barren which was considered a disgrace. Leah had six boys and a girl. She does this so Jacob will love her. Rachel gets upset at Jacob and tells him to give her children or she will die in Genesis 30:1 and he tells her he doesn't have any control over the situation in verse 2. Despite her faithless acts, God gives her children. She was also a thief and a liar. She stole her father's idols and lied about it when they were moving in Genesis 31. When she died, they buried her in Bethlehem and Jacob marked her grave with a pillar.

RAHAB

The name Rahab is the Hebrew word רָחָב means "spacious" in Hebrew. She was born in 1213 BC and died 1113 BC at the age of 99. We find her story in the book of Joshua. She was actually a prostitute in Jericho. The city was fortified with a big wall and Joshua sent two spies inside and they stayed with Rahab. When the king found out, she hid them on the roof. Before they left to go back, she agreed to help them escape if the Lord would spare her and her family. They agreed if she hung a red rope outside her window and her family had to stay inside with her when the battle came and that she couldn't tell anyone. When they left, she lowered them down the city wall as her window was on the side of it. As you can tell, she wasn't stupid. How did the spies end up with her? She probably figured out what they were and got them to come to her house and hide them there. When the king's men came to her house and asked about them, she admitted they were there, but left before the city gates were shut. God spared her and her family's life because she kept her word. When you look at this as she was a prostitute living in a city that worshiped false gods, you don't think to yourself, "Faithful Follower of God." She's also a liar and a deceiver and God still blessed her for taking care of His people. She was the first Gentile that converted in the Bible and through her linage, came Jesus.

REBEKAH

The name Rebekah is the Hebrew word רִבְקָה means "captivating".
She was born to Bethuel, Abraham's nephew. I could not find
anything about her mother other than in Gen 24:28 when it
records that she ran to her mother's household. This was the
account of her being chosen by Abraham's servant, to marry Isaac.
Rebekah was a virgin according to verse 16 and becomes the wife
of Isaac. This was as important back then to God fearing people
as it is now. Isaac was her second cousin. They had twin sons
together, Esau and Jacob. This didn't happen right away. In fact,
Gen 25:21 says Rebekah was barren so Isaac prayed and God
granted his prayer. She gave birth to the first set of twins mentioned
in the Bible. In verse 22 it actually says that they fight in the womb.
When she asked the Lord why this was happening, He spoke a
prophecy to her about two nations inside of her in verse 23. The
older would serve the younger. When the twins were born, verse
26 states Isaac was 60 years old. Rebekah actually favored her
youngest Jacob because Isaac had favored Esau. So, she felt sorry
for Jacob and actually helped him deceive her husband by stealing
Esau's birth right. Gen 27:1-40. Once again, Rebekah helped Jacob
escape his doom by his brothers' hand in verse 41-46. God honored
Isaac's request to be a father and his son's fulfilled prophecy even
though Rebekah was deceitful in her actions.

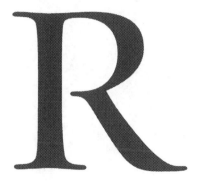

RUTH

The name Ruth means companion, friend and vision of beauty. Ruth was a Moabite and born around 1247 BC. She was the daughter of king Eglon, which would have made her a princess. She had a sister named Orpah. She was the wife of Boaz and the mother of Obed, which Obed had Jesse and Jesse had David, the king of Israel. Her story is an amazing one. She is one person in the Bible that doesn't dishonor the Lord. She in facts honors Him by leaving her people and moving with Naomi to take care of her. Naomi probably wasn't that old but she was alone and that was never good for a woman in those days. In those days, when a husband dies, then the brother takes his wife in but neither one of them had a brother-in-law alive so all they had was each other. Ruth would go out to glean the fields each day and she met Boaz, the owner of a field. He took a fancy to her because she was faithful to Naomi according to 2:11-12 and told her to glean only in his fields. He also made sure she had plenty to glean by telling his harvesters to drop extra for her to pick up each day. In 2:21 Naomi tells Ruth they are actually related. She talked Ruth into going to him one night in Ch 3 and laying down at his feet. This was actually a marriage proposal, but there was another they had to clear it with first because the other guy had dibs. In Ch 4, he gets the clearness and Ruth is his wife in verse 13. Life is good after that.

SAMSON

The name Samson comes from the Hebrew name שִׁמְשׁוֹן Shimshon, derived from שֶׁמֶשׁ shemesh meaning "sun". Most scholars give a birthdate around 1100 BC and he died in Judges 16:30. His father's name was Manoah and no name are given to his mother. He was raised a Nazirite according to Judges 13:5. His mother was given very strict instructions during her pregnancy and once he was born like not drinking any alcohol and not eating anything unclean. Once he was born, she wasn't allowed to cut his hair. According to verse 5, he would begin to deliver Israel out of the hand of the Philistines. In verse 24 he is born and in verse 25 he is an adult already. He wanted to marry a Philistine woman, which was outside his nation and his parents were upset because it was against God's law. He traveled to Timnah and on the way, a Lion attacks him and he kills it with his bare hands with the Spirit of the Lord according to 14:6. So we know he had superhuman strength. His wife ended up betrayed him. Samson had a habit of killing Philistines. Once he killed a 1000 of them with a jawbone of a donkey in 15:15. Samson went into sin a lot and he was easily taken in by Delilah when she tricked him into cutting his hair. By following after his own lusts, in the end it cost him his life. The upside was, even until the end, the Lord was with him. Samson prayed and the Lord gave his strength back when he needed it the most.

SAMUEL

The name Samuel is the Hebrew word שְׁמוּאֵל Shemu'el, which could mean either "name of God" or "God has heard". Samuel came from the tribe of Levi. He is the first of all prophets according to Acts 3:24. He is the last of the judges according to 1 Sam 7 and 12. Israel rejected the Judges because of their sinful life style. His birth is all over the place. The Bible doesn't give an exact date but most believe it was around 1170 BC because he became Judge around 1140 and held that for 40 years. His father was Elkanah and his mother was Hannah. She couldn't have children and prayed and God opened her womb but she promised God that she would dedicate Samuel according to 1 Sam 1:11. She kept that vow and Samuel was raised by Eli in the temple. In 1 Sam 3:7 the Lord had called to Samuel and he thought it was Eli. Then Eli said it is the Lord, go and find out what He wants. The Lord gave Samuel a prophecy and after that, his reputation spread all over Israel as a prophet. In 1 Sam 7:9-13, Samuel became the last judge when he instructed Israel to get rid of their false god's and turn back to the Lord or else they would fall to the Philistines. They did what he asked. He had two son's named Joel and Abijah which were wicked. He appointed them judges but the elders told Samuel they wanted a king instead. He went to the Lord and the Lord told him to grant their request but to not expect much better. Ch 25, He died.

S

SARAH

The name Sarah is the Hebrew word שָׂרָה meaning lady, princess, noblewoman. Sarah was born around 1986 BC and lived 127 years according to Genesis 23:1. She was from Ur, the land of the Chaldees, which were pagans. She was a beautiful woman according Genesis 12:11. She was the half-sister of Abram and his wife. They had the same father named Tehar but different mothers. In those days, marrying half siblings wasn't considered bad. When her and Abram were traveling, Abram had hidden the fact that they were married to keep from getting killed in Genesis 12 and in 20. He only told the half-truth. Sarah was also barren and of course this caused her stress. A woman that couldn't give her man children suffered cultural shame. Abram worried he wouldn't have an heir but God promised them they would have children. Sarah got impatient and gave Abram her maid servant Hagar to have a son, which he did and his name was Ishmael. This caused problems later. God change her name to Sarai in Genesis 17:15 which means "mother of nations". God still honored His promise to her by giving her a son. She was 90 according to Genesis 17:17. At first, she laughed when she heard this Genesis 18:9-15. This showed disrespect to the Lord. They had a son and named him Isaac which means "he laughs." Despite her disobedience, she is known as a faithful person. Hebrews 11:11, 1 Peter 3:5-6.

SAUL

The name Saul comes from the Hebrew name שָׁאוּל Sha'ul meaning "asked for, prayed for". According to Biography.com dated Apr 2, 2014, king Saul was born around 1130 BC in the land of Benjamin and became the first king of Israel around 1100 BC. Saul was about 30 years old when he became king according to the NET. He reigned for 40 years over Israel according to Acts 13:21. He had three sons named Jonathan, Ishvi, and Malchishua. He had two daughters named Merab and Michal. His wife's name was Ahinoam. King Saul was a great military leader. He led many victories and gained popularity, but as all great leaders, he started to do the wrong things in the eyes of the Lord. He performed a burnt offering in 1 Sam 13:9 that he wasn't supposed to. According to 1 Sam 10:8 he was supposed to wait seven days until Samuel was to come and instead, Saul made the offering. Because of this, Samuel told him that he was a foolish man and that the Lord has chosen someone else to be king. This didn't happen right away. In 1 Sam 15:3 he was given a task and he failed to honor the Lord again. He was told to totally destroy the Amalekites and all their livestock and he did not. He kept some of the best and allowed king Agag to live. The Lord told Samuel He regretted making Saul king. Samuel cried all night and the next day he questioned Saul. You can read the accounts in Ch 15, but bottom line, he was done as king and Samuel hacked king Agag into pieces in verse 33.

S

SOLOMON

The name Solomon is from the Hebrew name שְׁלֹמֹה Shelomoh,
which was derived from Hebrew שָׁלוֹם shalom meaning "peace".
Most can agree that he was born around 1010 BC and according
to 2 Sam 12:24, Solomon is the son of king David and Bathsheba.
He was around 20 years old when he became king of Israel it is
believed. He reigned for 40 years according to 1 Kings 11:42 when
he died. When he became king, the Lord asked him what he
wanted and all he asked for was wisdom and the Lord gave him
so much more according to 1 Kings 3. In chapter 4 he establishes
his administration. In chapter 5 he prepares to build a temple in
Jerusalem. In 6:1 it states that after 480 years of the people of Israel
coming out of Egypt, Solomon begins the building of the temple
to the Lord. According to verse 38, it took him seven years. In 7:1
he builds a house for himself which took 13 years. He had 700
wives and 300 concubines, which many of them were from other
countries and they brought their idol worship with them. During
this time Solomon fell away from the Lord and because of what
the Lord promised him, he did not take away the kingdom from
him. The Lord in 11:23 raised up adversaries against him and
caused trouble for him because of his disobedience. One thing I
learned about Solomon, you can start out on fire for the Lord, but
if you take your eyes off of Him, you will fall away. Stay connected.

ZERUBBABEL

The name Zerubbabel means "conceived and born in Babylon" from a contraction of either Assyrian-Babylonian Zəru Bābel "seed of Babylon" or Hebrew בָּבֶל זְרוּעַ Zərua'Bāvel "the one sown of Babylon". Zerubbabel was the grandson to king Jehoiachin. Zerubbabel father is known to be Shealtiel according to Ezra 3:2, 8; 5:2 and a few other places. His birthday is between 587 and 539 BC which in other words, no one really knows. He was the governor of Judah and was appointed to oversee the reconstruction of the Jerusalem temple, which Joshua the high priest was involved with. People that saw the foundation of the temple were upset to say the least because it was smaller than Solomon's temple. In Ezra 3:12 the prophet Haggai address this issue. He basically said to not sweat the small stuff. The Lord has big plans for the new temple. In 515 BC the temple was completed. The prophets Haggai and Zachariah saw that Zerubbabel was a descendant of David to include Jesus. The Lord declared that Zerubbabel would be chosen by Him in Haggai 2:20-23. Lord told him he would make him like a signet ring, which was an official stamp that each king had to seal documents. They were used to designate ownership or authority. Zerubbabel's name is erased from scripture before the temple is finished, but he is considered one of the greatest biblical heroes. The temple he oversaw still stood 500 years later when Jesus walked into it.

New Testament

PEOPLE

ANANIAS

The name Ananias comes from Ἀνανίας Hananias, the Greek form of HANANIAH which means Yahweh has been gracious. His birth is unknown but some believe he was born in Damascus and died in Eleutheropolis, Israel. He was known as a member of the church in Jerusalem and he was married to Sapphira. We know they were wealthy because the scripture states in Acts 4:34 *"Nor was there anyone among them who lacked; for all who were possessors of lands or houses sold them;"* Ananias, even though he was a follower of Christ, he still had some major issues with trusting the Lord with his money. In Acts 5 it says that they sold a portion of the land that they owned and kept back part of the proceeds. Later, Ananias went by himself and laid the money at the disciples' feet and acted like he did a great thing, but Peter asks him in verse 3 why Satan filled his heart and lied about how much he actually sold the land for. When Ananias heard this, he died right then. Then these young guys came and wrapped him up and buried him quick. They didn't even tell his wife what had happened. Then three hours later, Sapphira came in. Same thing, she lied about it and Peter said in verse 9, you see those guys there at the door, they're going to carry you out the same way they did your husband. Then she died. In verse 11 it states that a "great fear" came upon the church and all those who heard. I bet that didn't happen again. The funny thing is, Sapphira's husband was dead and buried and she had no idea.

ANDREW

The name Andrew comes from the English form of the Greek name Ανδρεας Andreas, which was derived from ανδρειος andreios meaning "manly, masculine", a derivative of ανηρ aner meaning "man". Andrew was a strong man. He had to be, he was a fisherman according to Matthew 4:18 and if you know anything about fisherman in that day, you know they used nets which could be extremely heavy if they got full. He was a disciple of Jesus along with his brother Simon Peter. He was from Galilee and some scholars believe he was born around 5 AD. They were originally disciples of John the Baptist and were there when John pointed Jesus out to them as the Lamb of God according to John 1:35-42. In this scripture, Andrew and Peter was able to spend the day with Jesus and knew He was the Messiah as John had said. Why they didn't follow Jesus right then is they were not ready. When they were ready, Jesus called them. When Jesus called them, they dropped everything "immediately" to follow Him. In John 6:8 Andrew told Jesus that a boy had five barley loaves and two fish. Then he asked how this was going to feed everyone. He truly wanted to know. He had been with Jesus and seen things that He did so, he knew Jesus had a plan. Fourth century writings say he was crucified on an "X" shaped cross around 70 AD as a martyr. This would make sense because he didn't care who he spoke to about the Gospel.

Apollos

The name Apollos is the Greek word Ἀπολλώς meaning "to destroy". We have no idea when he was born or died. The history on him just says both happened in the 1ˢᵗ century. We do know he was an evangelist, a church leader and a friend to Paul. According to Acts 18:24 he was a Jew born at Alexandria. The scripture says he had been instructed in the way of the Lord; and being fervent in spirit, he spoke and taught accurately the things of the Lord, though he knew only the baptism of John. According to verses 26-28, once he learned the way of Jesus, he boldly preached the gospel and refuted the Jews publicly. As Apollos went about preaching, a following was growing in Corinth for him. Paul had to discuss how this wasn't healthy in 1 Cor 1:12-13. He states *"Now I say this, that each of you says, "I am of Paul," or "I am of Apollos," or "I am of Cephas," or "I am of Christ." 13 Is Christ divided? Was Paul crucified for you? Or were you baptized in the name of Paul?"* This wasn't any fault of Apollos. This happens even in the church today when I hear, "I go to Pastor Dave's church". Who's church? Don't you mean God's church. I get what they mean but I saw people leave a church when our pastor left. They followed him to the next church 300 miles away and said that God told them to go. There were 10 families that went. This was clear evidence of people following man and not God!

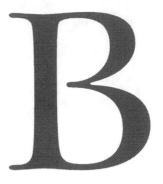

Barnabas

The name of Barnabas is the Greek form of an Aramaic name, which means according to Acts 4:36 Son of Encouragement. His birth name was actually Joseph. In the same verse it states that he was a Levite of the country of Cyprus. His birth is unknown and it is believed that he died in Salamis, Cyprus around 61 AD. We know that he put the kingdom of God ahead of himself because in verse 37 it states that he sold his land and brought it to the disciples' feet. This was a sign that he wanted more of God and less of himself. Barnabas was recognized by Paul because he was working to support himself without relying on the churches while he was on his ministry according to 1 Cor 9:6. Of course Paul did the same thing according to Acts 18:3. Maybe that is why he mentioned it, because they were of the same heart. Barnabas certainly loved Paul because he stuck up for him after Paul's conversion, which was still Saul at the time. The disciples in Jerusalem were scared of Paul because of what he was and Barnabas eased their mind in Acts 9:26-30. In Acts 13:1-3 Barnabas went on his first missionary trip with Paul to preach to the Gentiles. They did some great work together until they got into a disagreement about Mark coming along on the trip in Acts 15:36-41. Could you blame Paul though? Mark left them high and dry and so Paul didn't think he could trust Mark again. Instead, Mark and Barnabas went on without Paul to Cyprus.

CAIAPHAS

The name Caiaphas is a form of Aramaic. Here is the Greek word for his name; Καιαφας. I couldn't find a meaning for it but he was the Jewish high priest during Jesus' ministry and he was no fan of what Jesus was doing. There are conflicting reports of when he was born, but most agree he was born 18 BC and died between 44 to 46 AD. He was the son-in-law to Annas which was the former high priest. He was also a member of the Sadducees. They were normally rich people that held a high position. They were often involved with politics and according to most historic records, they help the majority seat of the Sanhedrin, which was the Jewish high court. Caiaphas was the ruler over this very court for 18 years. Sadducees didn't believe in the spiritual world or believed in anything after you died. If you were to compare them with the Pharisees, they were both very different. They didn't agree on government issues either. One thing they did agree on is that Jesus had to die. Jesus was brought in front of Caiaphas to stand trial and false witnesses testified but there wasn't enough evidence to put Him to death according to Matthew 26:59-60 so Caiaphas asked Him point blank in verse 63; *"I put You under oath by the living God: Tell us if You are the Christ, the Son of God!"* After Jesus answered him, that's all he needed to convict. The Savor of the world stood before him and he didn't see it. Instead, he called Jesus a blasphemer.

CORNELIUS

The name Cornelius comes from the Roman family name that possibly derives from the Latin element cornu meaning "horn". However, he was a Gentile and the first one to convert to Christianity according to Acts 10. He was a centurion in the Roman military in Caesarea according to Acts 10:1. A centurion was a Roman officer in charge of a hundred men. He was part of the Italian regiment. Normally, Roman religion was filled with false gods and Acts 10:2 was very clear, he had rejected that belief. He was a God-fearing man and well respected by the Jews according to Acts 10:22, so his belief in God was not hidden. It also wasn't a threat to anyone because he hadn't declared Jesus as King. That was an act of treason in that day. In Acts 10:3-7 Cornelius had a vision of God sending an angle to him stating He wanted Peter to come to his house. In Acts 10:34-48, Peter came to his house and preached the power of Jesus and in verse 43 he stated *"To Him all the prophets witness that, through His name, whoever believes in Him will receive remission of sins."* In verses 44-46 it says that the Holy Spirit was poured out on all who believed. Cornelius is responsible for Gentiles coming into the church from that day forward. Acts 10 is proof that the Gospel is for everyone. Cornelius was religious and still, that wasn't enough. He needed the saving grace of Jesus Christ.

ELIZABETH

The name Elizabeth came from the Greek form of the Hebrew name אֱלִישֶׁבַע Elisheva' meaning "my God is an oath", derived from the roots אֵל 'el referring to the Hebrew God and שָׁבַע shava' meaning "oath". She was born in the 1st century BC in Hebron. She married Zechariah and according to Luke 1:6, *"And they were both righteous before God, walking in all the commandments and ordinances of the Lord blameless."* This is an honor to be considered righteous. It doesn't matter what people think as long as the Lord is pleased. Elizabeth was a cousin to Mary, the mother of Jesus. But she was much older than Mary was. Luke 1:7 explains her being "advanced in years". This is mentioned to set the stage of how awesome God is. He sends the angel Gabriel to tell the couple that they are going to have a baby and to name him John. In Luke 1:24, when she found out she was pregnant, she didn't tell anyone for five months. Why didn't she tell anyone? Not sure but in verse 25 she explains God has removed her reproach or disgrace. In Jewish families, if you had children, it meant that God had found favor on you. Leviticus 26:9 says *"For I will look on you favorably and make you fruitful, multiply you and confirm My covenant with you."* When Mary came to her house and Elizabeth heard her greeting, she was filled with the Holy Spirit. She gave birth to John the Baptist, the one that prepared the way for Jesus.

HEROD ANTIPAS

The name Herod comes from the Greek name Ἡρωιδης Heroides, which probably means "song of the hero" from ἡρως heros meaning "hero, warrior" combined with ωιδη oide meaning "song, ode". He was born in Judea in 21 BC. Usually a last name comes second but, in this situation, Herod is considered the family name. As we know there are four different people in the Bible that are referred as Herod. This one is the son of Herod the Great which we will discuss next. According to Luke 3, Herod is the tetrarch of Galilee during the fifteenth year of the reign of Pontius Pilate, who is governor of Judea. According to Luke 3:18-20, John the Baptist rebukes Herod for his marriage to Herodias. He divorced his first wife to marry her, which was his brother's wife. Because of this, John goes to prison. According to Matthew 14:5 he wanted to kill John but he was afraid of the people. The people believed John was a prophet. But on Herod's birthday, he was tricked by his own words and had John's head brought in on a plate. In Luke 23, Herod finally faces Jesus and tries to get him to do things for him and Jesus refuses so he has Him beat, mocked and sent back to Pilate in verse 11. In verse 12, Pilate and Herod become friends, which they weren't before. Later Herod was exiled to Gaul because he was accused of conspiracy against the new Roman emperor by his nephew, Herod Agrippa. Antipas died 39 AD.

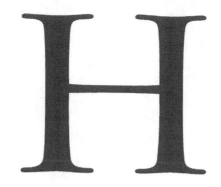

HEROD THE GREAT

Herod was born 75—73 BC in Edom, which was fitting since those people were of a wicked background. He was the king of Judea and had a reputation for slaughtering innocent people however, by many, he is praised for his work of rebuilding and upgrading the Temple of Jerusalem between 20–19 BC. He did this to gain popularity with the Jewish leaders. He didn't do anything new here. Cyrus did things like this and it worked. After that, the temple became known as Herod's temple. He actually got married in it to his wife Mariamne, which later he killed along with her two sons because he considered them rivals. This is the king that sent the Magi, which is the Greek word μάγος, ου, ὁ meaning astrologer or magician, to go look for Jesus and bring word back to him so he could go worship Him as well according to Matthew 2:7-8. Herod was upset about this because he was given the title, "King of the Jews" by the Emperor Augustus. He was given the order to destroy Judea and after three years, he did it in 36 BC. Herod knew the birth of Jesus had been recorded in prophecy so he called the scribes together to figure out the birth place. When the Magi did not return. He got angry and had all the children 2 years and under killed, but Jesus was spared because God had warned them to leave and go to Egypt. In 4 BC Herod died due to an illness so we know that Jesus was probably born around 6–4 BC. We talk about this when we study about Joseph, Jesus' father.

JAMES THE APOSTLE

The name James comes from the English form of the late Latin name Iacomus, which was derived from Ιακωβος Iakobos, the New Testament Greek form of the Hebrew name Ya'aqov. This James was a disciple of Jesus and the son of Zebedee. He was born in Galilee and was a fisherman. He was mending their nets with his brother John when he was called by Jesus to come follow Him in Matt 4:21-22. The scripture said that they immediately left the boat and their father and followed Jesus. Leaving their father just sitting there. This was the family business and livelihood and they left it. This is the effect Jesus had on people. To forsake everything for the Kingdom of God. He and his brother John were among the first to become disciples. Jesus referred to James and his brother in Mark 3:17 as "Sons of Thunder". What an honor to get a nickname from the Lord however, was this a compliment? In Luke 9:51-54 they wanted to call fire out of Heaven because Jesus wasn't welcomed into a home. They were fired up. Jesus turned and rebuked them. He was teaching them to love and not destroy. James continued with Jesus and was there for many of the events that happened such as, Jairus' daughter raised from the dead according to Luke 8:50-56. He was there on the Mount of Transfiguration (Matt 17:1-4) and when Jesus was in deep sorrow in the garden in Matt 26:36-37. James died as a martyr when in Acts 12:2 Herod Agrippa killed him with a sword.

JAMES THE BROTHER OF JESUS

James was born in Nazareth in the 1st century BC and is the author of the Book of James. It was written between 50 and 60 AD. He was never mentioned as one of Jesus' disciples but was His half-brother. He is often confused with James, the son of Zebedee. The interesting thing is, James was not a believer at first according to John 7:2-5. Living with Jesus, some say 30 years, which I'm not convinced of that because we don't know how old Jesus was when James was born but never the less, not seeing Jesus for who he was is odd to me. Jesus was a young boy without sin. Imagine that in your household, a brother that did no wrong. However, James was actually one of the first people to see Jesus alive according to 1 Corinthians 15:7 after the resurrection. It is not clear when James became a believer but he was in the upper room in Acts 1:14 so we know he became one. In fact, so much so, that he is known as a pillar in Galatians 2:9. He identifies himself as a servant of God in James 1:1. As you read his book, you see he is really concerned with Christians not doing what they are saying or believing. He actually warns in 1:22 by saying *"be doers of the word, and not hearers only, deceiving yourselves."* His book explains faith without works 2:14-26. He warns about an untamable tongue 3:1-12. Humility cures worldliness 4:7-10. Bring back the sinner 5:19-20. Scholars believe he died a martyr around 62 AD but I found no biblical evidence for that claim.

JOHN THE APOSTLE

The name John comes from the English form of Iohannes, the Latin form of the Greek name Ιωαννης Ioannes, itself derived from the Hebrew name יוֹחָנָן Yochanan meaning "YAHWEH is gracious", from the roots יוֹ yo referring to the Hebrew God and חָנַן chanan meaning "to be gracious". John was born 6 AD and is the brother of James, another disciple of Jesus. The scripture says that these two brothers acted immature in their early days when people rebuked Jesus. They wanted to call fire out of Heaven to destroy the Samaritans and Jesus had to teach them that he came to save men and not destroy according to Luke 9:51-55. They both had zeal for the Lord to say the least. They started out Disciples and became Apostles as they matured. The difference between the two is a disciple is a student of a mentor and an apostle is a messenger and ambassador. As you read further into the New Testament, you can see the level of maturity in all of the disciples. John wrote five books of the New Testament. The Book of John, 1, 2 and 3 John and the Book of Revelation. John was imprisoned for his faith on the Island of Patmos to work in the labor mines in 96 AD because of his faith. He started having vision of Jesus and wrote Revelation. He died peacefully in 98 AD in Ephesus after being freed most likely because he was an old man and couldn't work anymore. If that was the case, then he received a blessing because during the time, people that were enslaved and could no longer work, were killed.

JOHN THE BAPTIST

John the Baptist was born 6 months before Jesus was and they both were related according to Luke 1:36. He was born to Zacharias and Elizabeth which at that time, were older than most parents were. This made his birth a true miracle. John was actually filled with the Spirit in the womb. They were both Jewish parents and lived in the "hill country" of Judea. The angel Gabriel is the one that brought the message to Zacharias. What is awesome about this is, this was foretold 700 years before in Isaiah 40:3-5 and you would have thought he would have been excited to know; the prophecy was directed towards his family. John lived a rugged and simple life in the mountains of Judea. He wore clothes made from camel's hair and ate locusts and wild honey according to Matthew 3:4. John is known as "A voice of one calling". He refers to himself as this person in John 1:23. John was also the first prophet called by God since Malachi 400 years early. Jesus refers to John as a prophet in Matthew 11:9-11. John came to prepare the way for Jesus by preaching and baptizing for the remission of sins, which the Greek word is βάπτω (bap-tid'-zo) to dip repeatedly or to immerse. John had disciples before Jesus did, once Jesus was baptized by John (Matt 3:16), that was the start of Jesus ministry and the end of John's baptism. In the end, John was beheaded by Herod Antipas according to Matthew 14:1-10.

JOSEPH OF ARIMATHEA

The name Joseph comes from Ioseph, the Latin form of Greek Ιωσηφ Ioseph, which was from the Hebrew name יוֹסֵף Yosef meaning "he will add", from the root יָסַף yasaf. Just to be clear, this is not the earthly father of Jesus. He is called Joseph of Arimathea because of where he came from, which was in Judea. He is the one that loaned out his tomb to Jesus after He died. Joseph was very important because the body of Jesus would have ended up in the dump like all the other crucified people did if he hadn't convinced Pilate. How did he convince Pilate? He was a part of the Counsel or the Sanhedrin which was the group of Jewish leaders that wanted Jesus to be crucified, but when you read Luke 23:51, you see he was against this whole idea. He was a secret believer and follower of Jesus. He had a little pull with Pilate, but he was still taking a risk and a chance of ruining his reputation. Once he got the ok, him and Nicodemus buried Him in his tomb. I feel I need to add that Joseph was a wealthy man. We know this because poor people didn't have their own tombs. Joseph had no way of knowing that his choice to bury Jesus there fulfilled the prophecy that was prophesied hundreds of years before in Isaiah 53:9 unless he had read the text. You may hear claims about Joseph being an uncle of Jesus' mother or that he preached the gospel in other countries but the Bible doesn't support that. In fact, he is never mentioned after the burial of Jesus.

JOSEPH

This Joseph is the earthly father of Jesus. We all know the story about him wanting to put Mary away because she was pregnant and that he wasn't the father. So, instead of looking at the obvious, let's take a look at some other aspects of Joseph. His lineage goes all the way back to king David, (Matthew 1:1-17) which was 14 generations. He was a carpenter and passed that trade onto Jesus. He was a righteous man that obeyed God even when all things seemed hopeless. As far as when he was born, there isn't any real clear evidence of when that happened other than we know he was born in Bethlehem. Most scholars will agree he was in his early 20's when Jesus was born. According to some scholars, Jesus was born between 6 BC and 4 BC. The last time Joseph is mentioned is in Luke 2:41-52 when he and Mary found Jesus in the temple at the age of 12 with the teachers listening and asking questions. We know that Joseph was dead by the time Jesus started His ministry because every time Mary is mentioned during His ministry, she is alone. Mark 3:31-35. When Jesus was on the cross, John 19:26-27 states that Mary was taken to live with the only disciple that was at the foot of the cross, which most likely was the Apostle John. The custom was Joseph would have been in charge of the body, but instead it was Joseph of Arimathea that buried Jesus in his own tomb.

JUDAS ISCARIOT

The name Judas comes from the Greek word Ιουδας Ioudas, the Greek form of JUDAH. Iscariot is not his last name like so many people believe, it is another name for the city Kerioth, a city in Judea. North of Jerusalem about 30 miles according to Biblehub.com. He was the only Judean to join the group of Disciples. This was the son of Simon Iscariot according to John 13:26. Gotquestions.com makes an interesting statement that the Iscariot family could have come from the cadre of Sicarii which were assassins among the Jewish rebels which make since, since Judas' motives about money was always to steal it or obtain it. He betrays Jesus with 30 pieces of silver (Matt 27:3). Every story needs a "Bad Guy" and Judas fits that roll like a glove. People wonder why Jesus made him a Disciple when He knew what Judas was going to do from the beginning. Not only He knew, but he placed him in charge of the money as the treasurer. I Tim 6:10 teaches us that the love of money is the root of all kinds of evil. Do you think Jesus was teaching this lesson here? Judas was the one in John 12:4-6 that complained about Mary anointing Jesus with the oil because it could be sold and given to the poor even though that wasn't in his heart. Everything played out exactly how Jesus wanted it to. Some would argue that Judas did not act on freewill but someone had to betray Jesus, and since Judas had a reputation of being a thief, he was the best choice. We know he felt remorse in the end because in Matt 27:3 he tried to give it back. He died by hanging himself according to Matt 27:5.

LAZARUS

The name Lazarus is from the Greek word Λαζαρος Lazaros, a Greek form of ELEAZAR. His name means God has helped, past tense. He was born in Judea and lived in Bethany in 5 AD and dies the first time in 30 AD. No one knows when he died the second time. Scripture doesn't record if he was married or had children. We know he honored his sisters by given them a place to live. The Book of John (11:1-16) is the only book the records the account of Lazarus of Bethany. Now before we go to much further, there was a second Lazarus mentioned in the Bible. He was the one that sat at the gate and begged. He was full of sores and desired to be fed in Luke 16:19-31. Many thought this was a parable but Jesus gives specific names like Abraham so this was not a parable. The one we are looking into was Mary and Martha's brother. We know that Jesus was really close to Mary, Martha and Lazarus. We also know Lazarus got sick and died and Jesus didn't show up to heal him right away. In fact, when He heard the news, He stayed two more days at a place beyond Jordan (John 10:40) according to John 11:5-8. By the time Jesus got there, Lazarus had been dead for four days. Jesus did this on purpose because in those days, if you were in the tomb longer than three days, then they knew you weren't sleeping, you were truly dead. This was to show the power He had over dead, but it wouldn't be the last time He demonstrated this power. When Jesus arrived, He raised Lazarus from the dead.

LUKE

The name Luke is also the Latin name Lucas, from the Greek name Λουκας (Loukas) meaning "from Lucania". Luke was a doctor who left his profession to traveled with Paul. He joined Paul in Toras in Asia Minor during Paul's second missionary journey. He was born in Antioch, Syria in the 1ˢᵗ Century and he is the writer of the Book of Luke and Acts. He died at the age of 84 and no one seems to know if he was martyred or just died. Other scholars say he died in Boeotia and some say Greece. Who knows, but what we do know is Luke wasn't around Jesus and did not follow the teachings until after the resurrection of Christ. He was a Gentile and was not one of the original 12 Apostles. He also was not circumcised like the ones Paul names in Colossians 4:11. He was never married. The Greek name Luke only appears three times in the New Testament in Colossians 4:14, 2 Timothy 4:11 and in Philemon 24. We know he is very humble because he doesn't even name himself in either books as the author but Paul mentions him by name. Luke was a close friend of Paul. We know this because Paul refers to him as "the beloved physician" in Colossians 4:14. Luke also gives the most accurate account of Christ's ancestry. He traces it all the way back to Adam. The Book of Luke is the longest of all four gospels which makes since with all that history he records. Amazing since he never met Jesus.

Lydia

The name Lydia Λυδια in the Greek comes from the name Ludia, which means beautiful one, noble one or kind spirit. This is another person I chose that very little is known about who she is. She was originally from Thyatira but living in Philippi, which was a major city of the district of Macedonia when she met Paul on his second missionary trip according to Acts 16. She was known to be a merchant of fine purple linen. In verse 14 when Paul was preaching down by the river, it was there he met Lydia and she was a worshiper of God. Notice how the scripture mentions she was a worship of God but not Jesus until she heard Paul speak in the same verse. This is telling me that she believed the Pharisees teaching and not the teaching of Jesus until verse 14. In other words, she was living under the law and not the Gospel yet. It goes on to say that God opened her heart to hear. In verse 15, she and everyone that lived in her house was baptized. This would have included any servants that lived there, not just her family. Then the scripture goes on to say she would not take no for an answer when she asked them to stay as guests. She wanted them to know how much she believed; she actually did not want to let them leave. The scripture says she "begged" them to stay. This story reminds me of Cornelius in Acts 10. Like Lydia, he knew God but hadn't heard the Gospel yet. This was a divine appointment for her. I pray for those.

MARK

The name Mark is a form of Latin (MARCUS) used in several languages. Fun fact. He was actually called John Mark in Acts 12:12 but he is better known as Mark. He was born in Cyrene, Libya but his birth date is unknown. Saint Mark was the author of the second gospel in the New Testament which was actually written before Matthew's book. Most scholars are placing the writing to be around 55-59 AD. His book was the shortest of all the gospels with only 11,304 words when you consider the original language word count. It doesn't mean that it was any less Holy. I have talked to people that enjoyed reading his gospel more than the others because it was very detailed. Another fun fact is the word "euthus" is the Greek word for "immediately" and it is used 41 times in Mark primarily because Mark puts an emphasis on Jesus' servanthood and when something needed to be done, Jesus did it "euthus". He was not one of the 12 disciples but he was a companion of Barnabas his cousin and Paul during their first mission trip according to Acts 12:25. He didn't continue on once they came to Pamphylia. There is no biblical reference to this but he probably got freaked out because there was a lot of demonic stuff (Acts 13:4-12) that had happened and Mark might not have been use to that. Later, when Barnabas set out again, he took Mark with him and that is where Mark got his name, Mark the Evangelist.

MARTHA

The name Martha comes from Aramaic מַרְתָּא marta' meaning "the lady, the mistress", feminine form of מַר mar meaning "master". Martha lived in Bethany and was the older sister of Mary and Lazarus. We see her three times in the Bible. First time in Luke 10. She is more worried about "Works" and not the worship of the Lord like her sister Mary was. Now some would say Martha just wanted to give the Lord her best and He would appreciate that but when she started rebuking Jesus for allowing her sister to just sit there, Jesus defended Mary's actions. The second time we see Martha is in a much better light. Her faith is strong according to John 11:22. Lazarus had been dead for four days and she said that whatever Jesus asked for, God would give. It was believed in those days once a person had been dead over three days, they weren't coming back. That is why some people say Jesus probably waited four days to make sure he was good and dead. The third time we see Martha is in John 12 when she was serving again in the capacity of fixing a big dinner for everyone. When we see Martha two of the three times in scripture, we notice she is hosting dinners in her house, which seems to be a big house. Then Mary brings very expensive oil out to anoint Jesus' feet which would have been a year's wages, we get the idea they had money. So, rich people can still love and serve the Lord.

Mary, the Mother of Jesus

Mary is the English form of Maria, the Latin form of the New Testament Greek names Μαριαμ Mariam and Μαρια Maria - the spellings are interchangeable - which were from Hebrew מִרְיָם Miryam, a name borne by the sister of Moses in the Old Testament. There isn't a lot that is told about her but what we do know she was of the tribe of Judah and came from the family of David according to Luke 1:32. She was born in the 1st century BC. Most likely around 19 BC and died around 48 AD. Scholars have debated her age when she gave birth to Jesus. Was she 15 or 16? In Jewish customs young women could be wed as early as 12 but wouldn't have sex until they were 16 or even older. Whether she was 15 or 16, her spiritual level is where it needed to be whether she knew it or not. We do know she had four other sons. James, Joseph, Simon and Jude. She was related to Elisabeth by marriage which she came from the family of Aaron. She had been living in Nazareth with her parents when the angel Gabriel came to her to tell her she was going to be the mother of the Jesus. By this, we know she didn't come from a rich family. To jump ahead to when Jesus was on the cross, she was standing there with John the disciple. She was also there with a few disciples when the Holy Spirit came upon them at Pentecost.

MARY MAGDALENE

I have often wondered why this Mary had a last name and it wasn't that she had a last name, but that she was actually from a small village on the Sea of Galilee called Magdala, which means "tower" in the Hebrew. (Μαγδαληνη) If you don't remember who she is, she was the one that Jesus healed of demons and then she, like many women, traveled with Jesus and His disciples into Galilee. She is also known as the sinner woman who anoints Jesus with her tears and is forgiven by Him in Luke 7:36-50. Mary is mentioned in all four of the gospels unlike most people. She was at the foot of the cross, John 19:25, and at the tomb, Mark 15:40. She was one of the women who told the disciples what they saw, Luke 24:10-11, which they did not believe them. The Apostles believed them to be idle tales. The interesting thing is there is no evidence in the Bible to support that she was a prostitute. People just assumed she was because it has been adopted by the church. The earliest writings that mention this is when Pope Gregory I in 604 AD preaches a sermon that suggested both Mary of Bethany and Mary Magdalene had been ladies of the house as one would put it. From then on, the church taught it. Just because something has been preached for hundreds, even thousands of years, doesn't make it the gospel. People tend to believe things about the Holy Ghost and Speaking in Tongues that isn't in the Bible. It becomes fact the longer it's preached.

M

MARY, SISTER OF MARTHA

Mary is the sister of Martha and is often times referred to as Mary of Bethany. Very little is talked about when it comes to this Mary. It is in Luke 10:38-42 where we see Mary is choosing to be close to Jesus instead of "working" like her sister Martha was. In fact, Martha rebukes Jesus because of this but Jesus says it is better to hear Him then doing "Good Works". Good works do not save you. Ephe 2:8-9. This is the first account of three that is mentioned in the Bible about Mary. The second time we see Mary is when Jesus comes to raise her brother Lazarus from the dead. She runs to Jesus with her eyes filled with tears in John 11, and is heartbroken, but Jesus cries with her and comforts her all the while knowing she would be crying tears of joy soon. Then in John 12:1-8 where we see Mary taking a whole pint of very expensive perfume made from Spikenard and pouring it on Jesus' feet and wiping it with her hair. This perfume was worth a year's wages. It is the color of roses and the plant grows in India. As you can see, Mary loves Jesus so much she wants to serve His physical need by washing His feet. She would sit by His feet all the time to hear every word He spoke. This was a way of honoring Him. She was criticized for this by Judas, but just like she did when Martha criticized her, she stayed silent and allowed the Lord to defend her. We can take a lesson from this. Satan will attack and the Lord will defend. Just stay silent when the Lord tells you to.

MATTHEW

The name Matthew is the English form of Ματθαιος Matthaios, which was a Greek form of the Hebrew name מַתִּתְיָהוּ Mattityahu meaning "gift of YAHWEH", from the roots מַתָּן mattan meaning "gift" and יָה yah referring to the Hebrew God. His name was originally Levi. We know this because Luke attributes a banquet to Levi and in the book of Matthew, to Matthew. Matthew was born in Palestine in the 1st century and was a tax collector according to Matt 9:9. In the same verse Jesus saw him in his office and said, "Follow Me" and he got up and left his source of riches, security, and comfort for hardship of not knowing when he would get his next meal. Tax collectors were considered sinners in those days. They were hated by their own people because they worked for the Roman government and enriched themselves by collecting more taxes then what was required. You would ruin your creditability by associating with them. He was one of the 12 apostles and the writer of the book of Matthew. It's often believed that Matthew's book was written first because it comes first in the new testament but Mark was actually first and no one really knows when the book of Matthew was written but most can agree it was written in the 70's. There is also some debate on if he was a martyr or not because no one knows how he died but we know he died in Ethiopia.

NATHANAEL

The name Nathanael comes from the Hebrew name נְתַנְאֵל Netan'el meaning "God has given", from the elements נָתַן natan meaning "to give" and אֵל' 'el meaning "God". It is believed that Nathanael was born in the first century according to most scholars. He was one of the twelve disciples called by Jesus in John 1:43. He was from Cana in Galilee according to John 21:2 and was introduced to Jesus by his friend Philip. What is interesting to note is he was one of the first to say Jesus was the Son of God in John 1:49. We often remember Peter declaring Jesus being the Son of God in Matthew 16:16 because Peter was one of the first to deny Him as well, but we hear little about Nathanael stepping up as well. Another interesting note is John is the only Gospel that mentions him but the other three gospels identify him as Bartholomew. There is that second name thing again. Remember the quote, "Nazareth! Can anything good come from there?" John 1:46, That was Nathanael that said that. This was understandable since Nazareth was so small, about 500 people at the time and had nothing to offer anyone. To be called a Nazarene was like being called a Hick, Redneck or Inbreed. Once he saw Jesus and Jesus said to him *"Here truly is an Israelite in whom there is no deceit"* vs 47, he knew this was Jesus, the Son of God vs 49. He was martyred in Armenia, being either decapitated or skinned alive.

NICODEMUS

The name Nicodemus is from the Greek name Νικοδημος Nikodemos meaning "victory of the people", derived from Greek νικη nike meaning "victory" and δημος demos meaning "the people". In John 3:1 he is recognized as a Pharisee, a ruler of the Jews. He spoke to Jesus about how a man can be born again once he is old and Jesus explained it using the Old Testament in Numbers 4-9. Some believe Nicodemus was asking these questions to find out what Jesus would say, but the Lord knew his heart. He didn't go to spy on Jesus. He was honestly seeking Him. Later in John 7:50-51, he tries to get the Pharisees to understand what they were doing was wrong according to their own law. Then, once Jesus was crucified, he helped Joseph of Arimathea in giving Jesus a traditional Jewish burial according to John 19:39 by wrapping Him in stripes of linen with spices. He brought a mixture of myrrh and aloes. The scripture says 100 pounds of it. This was an extreme amount because it was custom to use 20 pounds. This would have been equal to about $150,000 to $175,000 in today's amount. Why so much? The only thing that comes to mind is Nicodemus loved the Lord so much, he wanted to make sure people couldn't smell the Lord while He laid in His tomb. You may wonder where he got the money. Pharisees were rich and he was a ruler so it stands to reason he would have the money to honor the Lord. I know the Lord appreciated his heart.

PAUL

The name Paul comes from the Roman family name Paulus, which meant "small" or "humble" in Latin. He was born with the name Saul in 6 AD as a Roman citizen to Jewish parents in Tarsus which is eastern Turkey now. He wrote most of the New Testament. From 20-30 AD he studied the Torah in Jerusalem with Gamaliel and becomes a Pharisee. Because of his schooling, he beliefs that the teachings of Jesus are false and starts killing Christians from 30-33 AD in Jerusalem and Judea. He is converted by Christ in 33 AD on the road to Damascus and loses his sight. Later, Jesus tells Ananias to find Saul and restore his sight in Damascus. He goes to Damascus to preach the Gospel in 36 AD and leaves about the same time to go to Jerusalem and meets with the Apostles. So, when was his name changed if it didn't happen on the road like we are taught in Sunday school? According to Acts 13:9 *"Then Saul, who also is called Paul, filled with the Holy Spirit, looked intently at him"*. This was a common thing to have two names. We all just believed once Saul was converted, his name changed. This is simply not true because then no one would have known him. Ananias helped the disciples to understand that Saul had changed. The miracle here is if a Pharisee can come to Christ, anyone can. Paul's life is too complex to put everything down here. Just know that he wasn't perfect either. In Romans 7:15-20 he makes statements about the things he wants to do; he doesn't do. He is referring to doing the right thing. Even the writer of most of the New Testament had his struggles.

PETER

The name Peter derives from the Greek word Πετρος which is Petros meaning "stone". Peter was born in Bethsaida in the year 1 BC and died around 67 AD. His name was actually Simon. Jesus was the one who changed it to Peter. Peter means rock and in Matthew 16:18 *"And I also say to you that you are Peter, and on this rock, I will build My church, and the gates of Hades shall not prevail against it."* When you read about Peter, you think this could never happen based on how he started out as a disciple. Let's look at his life before his walk with Christ. He was a Galilean fisherman and Andrews brother. He was married and a follower of John the Baptist. He was a sinful man and was ashamed of it when he saw Jesus according to Luke 5:6-8. Fisherman at the time were not thought of as clean men. They cussed a lot and had bad tempers. May this be why James and John were called the Sons of Thunder. Peter had all these issues and they carried into his discipleship with Christ when he was always sticking his foot in his mouth. But he didn't hesitate when Jesus asked both of them to follow Him. They dropped their nets and went. Peter always spoke up and Jesus had to talk him down. He cut off the ear of the Roman soldier in the garden and then later denied Christ three times. Peter ended up being the "Rock" that Christ built His church on in Matt 16:18.

PHILEMON

The name Philemon is Φιλημων which means affectionate in the Greek, a derivative of φιλημα philema meaning "kiss". Philemon was a rich Roman citizen from Colossae and he met Paul when Philemon had traveled to Ephesus. It was there that Philemon became a follower of Jesus and later, became a church leader in Colossae. During this time, Philemon owned slaves and one of them was named Onesimus. There was a dispute between the two of them which I could not find any information on what that was but whatever it was, it caused Onesimus to escape. Later in Philemon 1:8, Onesimus goes to Paul in prison and asks for help because now he is an escaped convict and under Roman law this meant imprisonment. During that time, he became a follower of Jesus as well as a servant of Paul. So, to make a short story a little shorter. Paul sends word to Philemon asking him to not only forgive Onesimus, but to welcome him back to Colossae as an equal and a fellow family member according to 1:17. This kind of thing did not happen in the Roman society. You didn't free a slave and then make them your equal. It actually would cause other slave owners to be upset for the fear that their slaves would expect the same treatment. Paul says to him if you are truly a partner with me, you will do this and if he owes you anything, charge it to me and I will pay it according to 1:18. Sounds like what Christ did on the Cross.

PHILIP THE APOSTLE

Who was Philip? He was one of Jesus' 12 disciples. His name in the Greek is Φιλιππος (Philippos) meaning "friend of horses". Philip was a missionary to Greece, Syria, and Phrygia. Philip the Apostle was frequently confused with Philip the Evangelist. He is also known as Philip the Deacon, which confused me when I was researching this. When you read in Acts of Philip and letter from Peter to Philip, it becomes difficult to separate the two. He was one of those people that Jesus personally called to be a disciple which there were only six that Jesus did that with. Not every disciple was approached by Jesus. Philip brought Nathanael; Peter brought Andrew. But in this case, Jesus went to Philip according to John 1:43. *"The following day Jesus wanted to go to Galilee, and He found Philip and said to him, "Follow Me."* Philip had been a disciple of John the Baptist and was from the town of Bethsaida in Galilee, which according to John 1:44, so was Andrew and Peter. Philip was the one who said that 200 denarii worth of bread would not be enough for each of them to get a little according to John 6:7, which 1 denarii compared to USD would be close to $10 or a day's wage. In other words, Philip was saying, almost a years' worth of wages wouldn't even feed all 5000. Philip died a Martyr by impaled with iron hooks and hung upside down. Extremely cruel but for him, rewarding!!!

PHILIP THE EVANGELIST

After studying Philip the Apostle, I realized that Philip the Evangelist was a different person altogether. I have been a Christian most of my life and it took writing this book to realize that. This Philip is first mentioned when the Hebrew and Hellenistic disciples get into a dispute in Acts 6. Philip is also the one that is in charge of the daily distribution of food and alms so that no one gets suspicious of partiality, which makes since, since he was one of the seven appointed by the apostles to take care of the widows and the needy according to Acts 6:1-6. He also went into Samaria to preach and perform miracles in Acts 8:4-6. He witnessed to Simon the magician and he became a Christian in Acts 8:9-13. Between verse 26-39 of that same chapter, an angel of the Lord sends word to Philip to meet up with a man of Ethiopia, a eunuch of great authority. Philip goes and he runs up to him and sees he is reading the writings of the prophet Isaiah. Philip says, "Do you understand what you are reading?" He said no, climb up here and teach me and Philip did and he baptized him in verse 38. About 18 or 19 years later, we see that Philip ended up living in Caesarea and according to Acts 21:9, this is where Paul and his companions had stayed while they were traveling. The scripture doesn't mention anything else about him except that he had four daughters that were virgin and had the gift of prophecy. What a neat man.

PILATE

We know him as Pontius Pilate. In the Greek it is the word Πιλᾶτος, ου, ὁ. The name actually comes from Latin origin. He was a Roman procurator of Judea around 26-36 AD. At the time, he actually was serving under Emperor Tiberius who took over for Augustus in 14 AD. He was the one who appointed Pilate as governor of Judea. We all have heard the story of Jesus and the roll Pilate played during His crucifixion but what people tend to forget is his wife told him to leave this matter alone in Matt 27:19. She had bad dreams about this. Fun Fact, in the summer of 1961, an Italian archaeologist led by Dr. Frova, dug up a piece of limestone that was 2.6 feet wide by 2.23 feet high, in a stadium in Caesarea. Before this, there were no manuscripts in existence that could prove that Pilate had ever existed. The stone was a dedication to Tiberius Caesar. This is how it was laid out. Line One: TIBERIEUM, Line Two: (PON) TIUS, Line Three: (PRAEF) ECTUS IUDA (EAE). You can see replica's in museums but the original is in the Israel Museum in Jerusalem. Another fun fact is along with the stone, there were a few bronze coins that had been made between 29-32 AD by Pontius Pilate. The family name Pontius tells us that there was a tribe of Pontii. It was one of the most famous of the ancient Samnite names. Scholars are not sure of the name but many believe that it meant "armed with a spear or a javelin".

PRISCILLA

Her name means "worthy, or venerable," as belonging to the good old time. She was a Christian woman living in the time after Jesus left his disciples in charge of spreading the gospel. Scripture doesn't talk about her back ground except she and her husband had come from Italy according to Acts 18:2. She was born in Pontus. She was a Jew of Asia-Minor. She was expelled by Claudius from Rome, and in Corinth, Priscilla became the honored and much-loved friend of Paul. In fact, she was most distinguished among his fellow-helpers in the cause of Christ. As Priscilla is always paired with her husband Aquila, it is difficult to separate her from him since their two hearts beat as one. They were very much in love and in ministry together. They are never mentioned apart. Some people actually believe she was stronger and more outgoing then he was. I couldn't find anything that stated she had children so we are going to assume she was childless. As far as what they did for a living, Luke states they were tentmakers in Acts 18:3. I could imagine all three of them sitting in a tent shop discussing their next trip as they are making tents. The scripture says that Paul had supported himself and in verse 4 he would "reasoned in the synagogue every sabbath, and persuaded the Jews and the Greeks". As lay ministers, we do need to work to support our calling most of the time. I would love to be supported but our mission field is at our work.

SILAS

His name in the Greek Σιλας probably a short form of Silvanus. This is the name of a companion of Saint Paul in the New Testament. Paul refers to him as Silvanus in his epistles, though it is possible that Silas was in fact a Greek form of the Hebrew name Saul (via Aramaic). It means "wood". A prominent member of the church at Jerusalem; also called Silvanus. He and Judas, surnamed Barsabas, were chosen by the church there to accompany Paul on his return to Antioch from the council of the apostles and elders in Acts 15:22, as bearers of the decree adopted by the council. He assisted Paul there in his evangelistic labors, and was also chosen by him to be his companion on his second missionary tour in Acts 16:19-24. He is referred to in the epistles under the name of Silvanus 2 Corinthians 1:19 KJV. According to Encyclopedia Britannica, he was probably born in Rome and died 50 AD. In Acts 15:22-40 we learn that he is one of the "chief among the brethren". A leader in the church. It is here that we learn that he was also one of the "chosen men" to go to the Gentile Christians in Antioch and Syria and Cilicia to speak about how the Law of Moses was not to be observed by the Gentile Christians. While Silas was with Paul, many came to know Christ. Achaicus (1 Cor 16:17), Chloe (1 Cor 1:11) Crispus (Acts 18:8), Erastus (Rom 16:23), Fortunatus (1 Cor 16:17), Gaius (1 Cor 1:14) to just name a few.

STEPHEN

Stephen was born around 5 AD and stoned to death for condemning the Jewish temple in 36 AD. He was considered the first martyr in Christian theology. Acts 6:5 introduces him as a faithful man of God "a man full of faith and of the Holy Spirit." Nothing is known about the personal life of Stephen—his parents, his siblings, or whether he had a wife or children; however, what is known about him is what is truly important. He was faithful, even when faced with certain death. He was tasked with feeding the widows. He was full of God's grace and power, performed great wonders and signs among the people according to Acts 6:8. He was extremely wise in the Lord and when an issue came up between him and the others, they could not handle an argument with him because of his wisdom. So, they falsely accused him and labeled him as a blasphemer and had him arrested according to Acts 6:11-14. Stephen was not concerned about his earthly position. Instead, he stood firmly on the side of Jesus Christ, no matter what could happen. Stephen spoke to the Jews about their disbelief in Christ and told them how they would suffer for it. It wasn't taken well. He reminded the Jews of everything God had done for them. This just upset them even more. So, they carried out the penalty for blaspheming which was being Stoned to death. Before he died, he told them he could see Jesus at the right hand of God. This probably infuriated them even more because he claimed to see Jesus sitting at God's right hand.

THOMAS

Thomas was one of the twelve disciples. He was born in the 1st century AD and died 53 AD. He was also called Didymus according to John 11:16; which is the Greek equivalent of the Hebrew name "twin." This would lead many to think he was a twin. Unfortunately, he is mostly known as we learned in Sunday School, as "Doubting Thomas" according to John 20:25; *The other disciples therefore said to him, "We have seen the Lord." So, he said to them, "Unless I see in His hands the print of the nails, and put my finger into the print of the nails, and put my hand into His side, I will not believe."* Thomas was also one to ask questions when the others wouldn't. In John 14:5 he asked the Lord where He was going and how could they know the way when Jesus told them He was going to prepare a place for them. The other disciples might have been thinking the same thing but Thomas wasn't' shy about asking. Thomas was actually really brave. He was willing to die with Christ in Jerusalem according to John 11:16. The other disciples like Peter, either disappeared or denied him. So, to place the term "Doubting Thomas" on him isn't really that fair when the other disciples weren't much better. History tells us that Thomas traveled outside of the Roman Empire as a missionary, possibly as far away as India to preach the gospel, which is yet another indication of Thomas' boldness.

TIMOTHY

The English form of the Greek name Τιμοθεος (Timotheos) meaning "honouring God", derived from τιμαω (timao) "to honour" and θεος (theos) "god". Timothy was a disciple of Paul on his missionary journeys. Basically, he was being taught by Paul. Paul had written two letters to Timothy that are in the New Testament called 1 and 2 Timothy. Timothy was born around 17 AD as a native of Lystra, but was a true Greek. He died as a Martyr in Ephesus when he was 80 years old. His mother was a Jewess named Eunice. She later became a Jewish Christian according to 2 Tim 1:5. Not much is mentioned about his father other than he was a Greek Gentile. Probably because he never converted but there is no evidence of that. Paul was about 48 when he met Timothy. It is speculated that Timothy was in his early 20's when Paul decided to take him on his travels preaching the Gospel. But before they could go anywhere, Timothy had to be circumcised which Paul paid for. Which when you read about Titus, Paul refused to have him circumcised because it wasn't necessary for salvation. But Paul made Timothy do it because according to 1 Corinthians 9:20, in order to minister to the Jews, he needed to become a Jew. This doesn't mean you do drugs to minister to a druggy, but you better not dress in a suit and tie to go down to skid row to minister, they won't except you.

Titus

The name Titus comes from a Latin origin "title of honor". He was born 39 AD in Rome, but was a native of Greece and was known as a Gentile by birth and was converted by Paul to the Christian faith. He died 133 AD at the age of 94 and was buried in Crete. His father's name was Titus Flavius Vespasianus—commonly known as Vespasian. Titus was one of Paul's most trusted associates, but not the writer of the book of Titus, Paul was. He traveled around with Paul starting with Jerusalem to help settle a dispute about being circumcised. Then Paul sent him to Corinth to settle disputes there that had taken place in the church. Then he went on to Macedonia to inform Paul of how things were going in that city and Paul was pleased with the information he gave. Paul asked him to go back to Corinth and carry back with him Paul's second Epistle to the Corinthians. The purpose of this epistle is to show the qualities a bishop should have. It was Titus' job to go to the isle of Crete and ordain priests and bishops. The last mention of Titus in the Bible indicates that he was with Paul during Paul's final Roman imprisonment. From Rome, Titus was sent to evangelize Dalmatia (2 Timothy 4:10), an area which later became known as Yugoslavia and is now called Serbia and Montenegro.

ZACCHAEUS

The name Zacchaeus means, "Pure", it is the Greek name Ζακχαιος. He was a tax collector in Jericho who gave half of his possessions to charity. He was born in the 1st Century AD. Zacchaeus was also a descendant of Abraham. According to Luke 19:1-10, he heard Jesus was coming so he went to see Him, but because he was so short, he ran ahead of the crowd and climbed a sycamore tree so he could see Jesus. He didn't think he was worthy enough to meet Him but he still wanted to see Jesus. When Jesus saw him, He told him to hurry down and Jesus would stay at his house that night. This would be the same as you meeting a movie star and the movie star asking you to come and hang out in their dressing room. That made him really happy but everyone else was mad because they figured him for a sinner. Remember, he was a tax collector and that means "Sinner" and hated by all, especially in 1st century Jewish culture. When he told Jesus he gave half of his earnings to the poor, Jesus said that salvation had come to that house in Luke 19:8-9. Zacchaeus even went as far as to say if he had cheated anyone out of anything, he would pay them back four times what he took. This passage shows that even rich people can come to the Lord. Keep praying for your loved ones that feel they don't need Jesus because they are alright at the moment.

ZACHARIAS

The name Zacharias comes from the Hebrew name זְכַרְיָה Zekharyah meaning "Yahweh remembers", referring to the Hebrew God. His name is also spelled Zechariah but the KJV uses Zacharias. He was born in the 1st Century BC and died 12 AD. His home was in the hill country of Judea in Israel. According to Luke 1:13, he is John the Baptist' father. He was a priest and according to 1 Chr 23:13, a priest was someone who offered sacrifices and did work for the Lord in the temple. Zacharias came from the tribe of Levi. He followed the law of Moses and was considered a righteous man. Luke 1:6 explains him as blameless when it came to the Torah. In Luke 11:1, Zacharias is actually the first one that an angel spoke to in the New Testament chronologically. Zacharias was in the temple when an angel Gabriel appears and tells him that his wife will bear a son: one who will go before Jesus. Because of his disbelief, the angel tells him he would not be able to speak until the prophecy was fulfilled according to Luke 1:19-20. This conversation would have taken place before Mary's and Joseph's visit from the angel Gabriel announcing the coming birth of Christ. He was an old man and had no children. This normally would have meant that the family line would have ended. It did anyway because John never had children, but Zacharias had to have been very happy with the fact of having a child.

CONCLUSION

When studying the people of the Bible, remember the times they lived in. They worked hard, worshiped with all their heart and or disobeyed with all their heart and God gave them their just due for their actions. Romans 6:23 states *"For the wages of sin is death; but the gift of God is eternal life through Jesus Christ our Lord."* The word "wages" means what you have earned. If you sow bad seed, you will reap the bad harvest. If you sow good seed, good things will come from your hard work. In everything I do, I do for the glory of God. I do without expecting payment for it. That is why all the profits that come from this book will go to PEC so that this ministry will continue to grow even when I'm not the president anymore.

I hope you have enjoyed the brief study of each person and I hope it will encourage you to study deeper than what I went into here.

Follow along with me on my YouTube channel at "Pentecostal Evangelical Church"

May God Bless You.

Sincerely,

Rev. Justin Morris
General Bishop of the Pentecostal Evangelical Church

Rev. J.W. Morris
General Bishop/President
Pentecostal Evangelical Church
Website: www.pec.today

If you feel the call to be credentialed and you don't know where to start, please go onto our website and check us out. We have a valuable product that will enhance your ministry.

Rev. Justin Morris (SFC Retired) is a 25-year vet.

References

Thomas Nelson Study Bible

Bible Timeline with World History

All Greek and Hebrew names were found from "Behind the Name" website https://www.behindthename.com/

Adam, Benner, J. A., Ancient Hebrew Research Center

Let Me Die the Death of the Righteous, (2019), Jackson. W., Christian Courier

Historical Evidence Belshazzar,

(2013), http://www.biblehistory.net/newsletter/belshazzardariusmede.htm

Silas, (2019) Encyclopedia Britannica, https://www.britannica.com/biography/Saint-Silas

Map of Kerioth (2019), Bible Hub, https://bibleatlas.org/kerioth.htm

Judas Iscariot, (2019), Got Questions, https://www.gotquestions.org/Judas-Iscariot.html

Printed in the United States
By Bookmasters